Age Gap
Relationships

The Attractions and Drawbacks of Choosing a Partner
Much Older or Younger than Yourself

Jill Pitkeathley and
David Emerson

Thorsons
An Imprint of HarperCollinsPublishers

Thorsons
An Imprint of HarperCollins *Publishers*
77–85 Fulham Palace Road,
Hammersmith, London W6 8JB
1160 Battery Street,
San Francisco, California 94111–1213

Published by Thorsons 1995

1 3 5 7 9 10 8 6 4 2

© Jill Pitkeathley and David Emerson 1996

Jill Pitkeathley and David Emerson assert the moral right to
be identified as the authors of this work

A catalogue record for this book is available from the British Library

ISBN 0 7225 3158 3

Typeset by Harper Phototypesetters Limited
Northampton, England
Printed in Great Britain by
HarperCollinsManufacturing Glasgow

Contents

Acknowledgements

We are indebted to many people for the help they gave us in writing this book. We want particularly to thank all those we interviewed who contributed their experiences and opinions. We are grateful that they were willing to share with us their feelings – sometimes distressing – and their joys and sorrows about their relationships. We also thank most warmly our families, friends and colleagues for being tolerant of our endless discussion about 'age gaps' and for contributing their thoughts. We hope those who read the book enjoy it as much as we enjoyed the research and writing.

Introduction

Headlines: Phil Collins has fallen for a Swiss millionaire's daughter who is just half his age. Glenn Close is to marry a man 12 years her junior ... Richard Gere is head over heels in love with a British model less than half his age ... A son 18 says his father's suicide was caused by mother's affair with much a younger man ... In the UK between 1979 and 1992 the number of men marrying a women at least 11 years older increased by one-third.

Why do people form relationships across a large age gap? What makes a woman marry a man 20–30 years older than herself? Why should a man choose a wife who is 15 years his senior? Sheila and Marion are sisters, two years apart in age; Sheila married a man 29 years older while Marion has lived for 15 years with a man 19 years her junior. Why did this happen? Sheila's situation is generally much more acceptable than Marion's, but why is this?

What do we mean by 'an age gap'? For the purposes of this book, we decided upon a minimum of a 15 year gap where the man is older and for gay relationships, and 10 years where it is the woman who is the older partner.

Judging by their treatment by the press and TV, age gap relationships are popularly viewed in terms of a younger partner replacing a parent, with the older one taking advantage of youthful inexperience; and all the while the scent of exploitation lingers in the air.

Yet if this was really true would so many couples maintain partnerships across the years? What do those people involved in such relationships get out of them? Is it that they all are a little bit peculiar? It is more probable they see lots of advantages in their relationship. But what exactly are these? And what about the disadvantages? We can now say, with certainty, that this popular view outlined above is far from the whole story – perhaps barely a part of the picture. The younger partners we met were sure that it was they who were getting the better deal. And, as for seeking someone parental, who *isn't* looking for such nurturing from their partners, whatever their age or sex?

Society sees these relationships as odd, abnormal in some way. Yet this conflicts with the commonly held view that love is all that matters in relationships. People always say 'Providing you have the right person nothing else matters; love conquers all. If you are in love, everything else is irrelevant.' Is this really so?

I always looked with slight distaste upon large age gap relationships, especially those in which the man was the older one. But when I met my own older man I lost all objectivity, as you do in love: our circumstances seemed unique, we didn't feel we fitted into any statistical pattern. (woman 22, man 43)

It may be a romantic notion, that one is capable of living, in love with anyone – no matter what the social, economic, age, attitude difference may be. We like to think these differences are, in love, arbitrary, imposed by society, and that the tension arises because there is a difference between what society expects and what we feel we can achieve ourselves.

I am aware that it is a statistical fact that marriages between people from a similar background and attitudes are the most likely to last – but a part of me wants to rebel against this. I think of myself as someone who is unlikely to marry the boy next door whereas I have friends, my

sister included, who always go out with men of their own .
ilk. I need different strokes.

Like many other discrepancies, the age gap only matters if
you want it to. I still like to think that love can subsume
any adversity, and triumph over perceived distances.

Well, this may suit our fantasies about how we would like our
relationships to be, but is it realistic? To achieve a successful
long-term relationship, more than love is needed. If love was
all that mattered, there'd be no questions to ask about age gap
relationships. Since there clearly is more to the issue, we
wanted to seek the views of people who are actually in such
relationships. We wanted to learn what they had to say and find
out why they got into their particular relationship in the first
place. What did they gain, or lose, in doing so? And what advice
would they give to others?

The popular press may frequently denigrate the age gap
relationship, but just because society may be disapproving, this
does not stop people embarking on them. Couples are willing
to face the apparent problems involved: it is difficult enough
maintaining any long-term relationship, let alone one which
appears to be inherently more risky.

How many such couples are there? In 1992 in the UK, 3,034
men married a woman at least 11 years older than themselves.
This represented a 32 per cent increase on the numbers in 1979,
and over the same period there was a 15 per cent decrease in the
number of all marriages. Marriages where the man was older
were even more popular. Over this same 13 year period there
were twice the number of marriages of women to men older by
16 years or more. Together in 1992 they comprised 2.9 per cent
of all marriages. Since there will be many more such couples
who are living together but not married, these figures underestimate the total number of all age gap relationships.

We have been in contact with many people who are or who
have been in age gap relationships – over 100 of them – and this

book reports these relationships in the words of those who have experienced them. It is aimed at all those who

- have had such a relationship
- are in one now
- are hesitating on the brink

In fact, it is for anyone who would welcome some perspective on their feelings and experiences.

We do not aim to be dogmatic or prescriptive. What we present are the feelings, experiences and opinions of those who know about age gap relationships. The gains set out are those gains they feel they have achieved through being in such 'peculiar' relationships. These include the 'opening of doors', the opening up of new perspectives and the concept of hybrid vigour. We also include their advice to others who may be thinking of embarking on a similar course. Whether that advice is to proceed with extreme caution or simply to 'go for it', we hope it may all be valuable. Having analysed the interviews and studied the statistics, we have come up with our own views about current trends and what we think the future may hold.

Our participants were older partners, younger partners, male, female, gay and straight, and of several different nationalities. All were eager to tell us about their experiences and we quote their words extensively. We guaranteed anonymity so names, locations and other identifying characteristics have been amended in the extracts quoted. We obviously cannot thank by name all those who gave time and thought to help us but we know who they are and hope they do too.

We are extremely grateful to them for their support and assistance. We hope that they, as well as anyone else who has experienced, or is contemplating, an age gap relationship, will find both what we and they have to say helpful.

I

How They Met

People in love, and those who have been in love, like to talk about how they met: we have all had the kind of conversation which begins, 'What did you really think the first time you saw me?' While our interviewees were no different from other couples in this, many of their relationships had begun much less conventionally. They were often open to approaches from a very different partner because of a particular set of circumstances:

- They might be seeking a more supportive kind of loving, because of distress from a previous relationship.
- They might be feeling vulnerable and looking for a relationship which can offer the kind of security that an equal age relationship might not provide.
- They might be outside their normal pattern of living – on holiday, on a course – which freed them to contemplate an age gap relationship where otherwise it would not have been a possibility or the opening meeting and gambits would never have presented themselves in the first place.

Here are some of the ways our interviewees' relationships started and then developed.

First Meetings

Against My Wishes

Many involved a strong element of being pursued – often against their initial wishes.

> One morning I jogged into his room by mistake, thinking it was the one to which I'd been assigned. We exchanged pleasantries but when I met him again later that day, he asked me out. I was quite shocked as I knew at once that I was at least 10 years older – 14 as it turned out – so I said something like, 'Don't be silly.' He persisted and I resisted for about three weeks.

> I had known him before we started going out together and hated him. He was a friend of my managing director's and we used to go to the pub and stuff and he kind of started orchestrating this campaign to get me to go out with him and I thought it was a total joke. I was 25 and he was 41 and I thought, 'This is absolutely ridiculous.' I'd never contemplated being interested in anyone of that age but he totally kind of wined and dined me and all that stuff and I thought, 'Oh well, maybe.'

Or the initial attraction was reluctant:

> He asked me to model for him and during our next few meetings I became increasingly attracted to him, but in a purely cerebral way. I was quite fascinated by him intellectually (he had a brilliant and original mind) but there was no corresponding physical desire on my part, though there clearly was on his. In the end the mental seduction was so great that I allowed a sexual relationship to develop but just, I think, as a means of consolidating something

with him. Physically it turned out to be the best relationship I've ever had in my life, though this may be partly
because women tend to come into full bloom sexually in
their mid-thirties.

Different Places, Different People

Some had broken out of their usual living pattern by taking a
holiday abroad, for example, and that had brought them into
contact with a different group of people.

> On the island, my friend and I asked at a house for a drink
> of water and he appeared from upstairs. The next night I
> met him in a bar and it went on from there. No one
> seemed to notice that he was 24 and I was an old lady of 47.

> At the age of 55 I took a teaching post in Kenya. I had been
> divorced from my husband for 12 years, my daughters
> were grown up and I felt free to follow my inclinations.
> Within two days of arrival I met Serge. He was barely 19
> but looked and acted a lot older. He was extremely attrac-
> tive but it was only when I realized that he was evidently
> attracted to me that I admitted this to myself. He took me
> round and showed me the sights and after barely a week
> our affair started. I thought he was ridiculously young but
> possibly the fact that I was staying in a new environment,
> entirely on my own for the first time in years, and had
> actually embarked on a kind of adventure, contributed to
> my attitude.

Student and Teacher

A large number of interviewees had met as pupil/teacher or
student/lecturer. Unsurprisingly, many women had been their
husband's students:

Michael was my teacher at school for three years. We started going out in the summer before my final year and lived together the year after that.

When I left the US for England and a term at a British campus, the last thing I expected was to meet a significant other. I was 21 when I arrived. Roger was 52, a widower and a lecturer on two of the courses I was taking. As the saying goes, our relationship was consummated in March and everything clicked.

I knew him when I was a student at art college: he was one of the tutors in my department. He was quite an aggressive tutor and I took a dislike to him right from the start, because he was heavy on the irony, which is not exactly what the first years need . . . By the time I left I thought, although he was fairly impossible, he had a warm heart, and I left my address card in his locker. I did not find him at all attractive, but thought it would be nice to keep in touch. Eight months later I was living with him.

But by no means were all the relationships those where it was the tutor who was the older partner, or the man:

I decided to go to a summer school because I was particularly interested in a class on Hardy. Giles was the tutor. I confess my heart leapt when I saw him because he looked like a young Lord Byron. I had just finished my relationship with Ralph, in which at the end he left me for a younger woman so I suppose I was feeling very unattractive and unwanted, and certainly that no man would ever look at me again. When he seemed to pay me special attention I thought I must be imagining it actually. I did not imagine he could ever want me as a girlfriend and it took us ages to get together because of my reluctance. (Kathryn 54, Giles 27)

Here is Anne-Marie:

> He was in my class at the further education college. I was always impressed with his thoughtfulness and the way he analysed the books we studied. Later he took to coming round to my house, and over a period of two years it has progressed from there. He is only 21 and I am 41 but there is a tenderness and beauty in our relationship which restores the hurt feelings we have both suffered in our lives. I have ceased even to think about what some people might call the abuse of my position as a teacher.

and Anthony:

> She was my headmaster's wife. I know that sounds like a risqué story. The headmaster was quite a bit older than her and she felt very inadequate because she had just had a baby and he, having had children from his first marriage, knew all about it whereas she could hardly cope. I expect she was drawn to me because I was young and gauche, and that in turn made her feel more grown-up.

and Nicola:

> I had taught Simon since he was 12 but it wasn't until the summer of his GCSEs that we became close. I taught him maths and between bouts of algebra we'd chat about last night's TV or our plans for the weekend. I didn't love my husband and I found Simon so easy to talk to. He used to ask me to join him and friends going bowling and I always had such a good time. But when my headmaster and his mother found out we spent time alone together, all hell broke loose and I was suspended.

The relationships were not always heterosexual, either. Hilary says:

We met when she came to London to study (theatre) and I was one of her teachers. I was almost 50, had been married for 16 years and had two children, both older than her. At that time I had been divorced and was in a relationship with a younger man. There was a very strong connection between us right from the start – no sexual contact though. It was two years later, after she had left the college, that our sexual relationship began. I was appalled – I had never had a lesbian lover before. That and the huge age difference were strong taboos for me.

What is Available

There was also an occasional element of 'what is available' when we looked for reasons as to why people chose an age gap partner. As one woman put it,

> By the time you get to your thirties you find most men are married and happily settled; most men of your own age, that is. What is on offer is either men much younger or older men who have got divorced or, more rarely, widowed and are on the second time around.

> Since I'd been divorced I'd had one rule: no married men. That limits the field. So younger men were available and free.

Many women who find themselves single in middle age have had the bruising experience of being left by their husband for a younger woman. Many of them react by feeling that, as one put it,

> I would never do to another woman what was done to me.

If they felt like this, they frequently found it quite difficult to meet another man in their age-group since, inevitably, most of them were married. It was for this reason that many of them 'found themselves' with younger men; not because they were especially seeking a younger partner but because they were the only ones available, though this was not necessarily a bad thing.

> We met at a single/divorced club when I was 55 and I told him, 'I'm one hell of a lot older than you.' 'So what,' he said and he never did ask my age until my 60th birthday.

Others met each other through various forms of advertising:

> I responded to this ad in the *Evening News*. I was drawn to his description of himself. I went to meet him somehow feeling the meeting was to be significant for me – as it proved to be.

> When I was 22 I heard this piece on the radio about this man sailing single-handed round the world. Asked if he ever got lonely he said, 'No but it would be nice to find a girl with the same interests to go along, too.' I wasn't actually interested in sailing but my life was in a mess and I thought it would be great to disappear into the pale blue yonder.

Some had some even more unusual beginnings:

> I was on holiday on a cruise with my husband and he was with a group of friends at our table.

> During the service at the new church, I turned round to shake hands and realized that the 'woman' was not . . . he was a practising transvestite.

One man actually met his future bride when she was a babe in arms!

As a lad of 19, riding a rather large Triumph motorcycle, I happened upon Lynne, Sandra's mother, sitting in the sidecar of a motorcycle combination outside a pub, cradling a small white bundle and drinking from a large glass of beer. In deference to the infant I did not accelerate from the road junction with my usual gusto.

Looking for Something Different

A few interviewees were actively looking for a particular type of relationship that an age gap partner would best satisfy. The recent proliferation of dating agencies perhaps attests to the numbers of people actively searching for a relationship of any kind. Although they may not be specifically seeking an age gap partner, they may well be looking for someone 'different':

By the age of 25 I had achieved my life's ambitions, thought that living alone was making me too self-centred, believed it would be 'good for me' to have to fit in with someone else and *not* always have my own way. So the purpose of marriage was character improvement rather than love, and you could say I found someone who fitted the bill in that I wanted someone older and interesting.

Even as a child I always latched on to older children and I felt more secure with older people. Our 21 year age gap follows this pattern, since perhaps it was a father-figure I enjoyed. The adage 'An old man's darling or a young man's slave' is probably correct, since I was certainly a replacement for his daughter who had recently left home.

Some of the people we spoke to felt that not only were they looking for something different but they were predisposed to this particular type of relationship. From our book, *Only Child*, we realized that many were prone to seeking age gap relationships:

> Because I was an only child and always in my parents' company, being attracted to men a fair bit older is out of a natural expectation that I would be around that age-group. Plus it links with needing my own space, so someone older will have a well-developed sense of their own space, which is consequently better for me.

> I have always been attracted to older men and they, in turn, have been attracted to me. I am much more interested in a man if he has at least 10 years on me. I often find this strange, although I never really question my reasons.

Repairing Damage

Where someone was coming from an insecure, difficult previous relationship, whether with their family or partner, they could be seeking a different type of relationship in order to repair emotional damage. An age gap partner is one likely solution. Here is Rebecca:

> I had just left a very unhappy home where my sister and I were treated like second-class citizens by my step-mother who didn't really want us, as well as my Dad (my mother had died) and so I was glad to leave home yet also terribly homesick at college – though I had no real home to be sick about, which possibly made this worse. I was also nursing a broken heart as I had split up with a serious boyfriend before coming to university. I spotted him on my first day at college, thought he looked interesting and was determined to 'get' him. I wasn't sure it was wise but

I wanted someone as I was lonely and I hadn't met anyone else interesting at the time.

and Penny:

My husband whom I married at 19 had an enormous ability to undermine me. From the length of my legs to the size of my intellect he was constantly telling me how I fell short of his ideal. It did me untold damage and I lost confidence completely. Somehow when I met Saul he repaired all that. It was partly of course because he was younger. It made me feel good that he fancied me and didn't think my legs were too short! But more than that. He seemed to view me and judge me by an entirely different set of standards, standards which had been set in a different time-frame and therefore not like those of my former husband.

Rebecca and Penny were seeking to develop their confidence by a new sort of intimacy; one which was secure and offered hope of re-evaluation away from the influence which had undermined them. The new and different relationship led them into a completely new emotional scenario.

Just the Same as Everyone!

Age gap couples are not a breed apart. Several of those we interviewed began their partnerships through the usual channels of pub:

We used to exchange banter in the pub until one day we chatted more seriously and we realized how much we had in common.

or hobbies:

I joined everything I could find to meet people when I first moved into the area, and met him in my evening class.

or work:

We spent a day working together, arranged to meet for lunch and from that moment I thought about more or less nothing else. Our relationship began slowly as he was wary of becoming involved with someone at work (and he was quite right – it's a lousy idea). After several lunches we went out to dinner and it started from there. He made me feel about 12 – I was terribly impressed by him and amazed he could find me interesting, and the whole thing absolutely astounded me.
(woman 27, man 43)

or through friends. Phillip, a gay man, describes it thus:

My older partner and I were introduced to each other by an even older friend of his who had tried – unsuccessfully – to pick me up a couple of weeks before. The introduction took place at a friend's flat. My head was definitely turned! A group of about seven or eight of us had drinks there before we set off in convoy for a night on the town. Douglas and I were the last to leave and never quite caught up with the main group. I found out later that I had been packaged as the mature youngster who might just pull off the impossible: Douglas in a stable and committed relationship!

The Next Steps

However they met, there seem to have been two distinct ways in which the relationship progressed. Sometimes it came as a bolt from the blue . . .

Our eyes met and I knew.

I knew immediately she was someone special.

I was immediately impressed by him and knew this was a precious moment.

When Pietro and I first saw each other, the attraction was mutual and instant. He was Portuguese and terribly handsome. We spent three months together as we were both working and living in the same area of Holland and camping in the same field.
(woman 22, man 44)

In these instances, awareness of the age gap only came upon them later, often when, as one put it,

I was hooked. If I had wanted to stop I couldn't have done so.

Alison did not actually know she was hooked, but she was, nonetheless:

He had been my teacher when I trained as a teacher. In some ways he was dreadful . . . going to his house for early morning tutorials I was often aware that he wasn't washed or shaved. His breath often smelled, and not only his breath. But somehow I was fascinated by him and even when I left college, I never quite forgot him. Years later my husband and I moved back into the area where I'd been at college and I heard of him again. I can't describe the feeling that came over me when I heard he'd been widowed quite recently. There was sadness for him but most of all this feeling that now we could be together and it felt as though that was what I had wanted all along though I had never acknowledged it before.

She went about achieving her objective with remarkable singlemindedness.

> I got in touch with another former student who I knew had kept in touch with him and got me and Bert invited for dinner at my friend's house, with him as another guest. Sitting at the table opposite him I could scarcely breathe for excitement. His shirt did not quite meet at the join with his trousers because there was a button missing and the combination was amazing for me . . . sad because he had no one to look after him, but excited to see the bare flesh. Before the coffee was served, I followed him into the kitchen when he helped to clear up, told him I'd always loved him and said I'd leave my husband immediately to be with him if he wanted me! It was dreadfully embarrassing for everyone and I blush to tell the story, but we were married to each other within six months of that night and are blissfully happy.

In some instances the consciousness of the other person as a potential sexual partner grew gradually, came upon them by degrees. In these instances, the age gap itself had prevented them having sexual thoughts about the other person.

> I never thought he could possibly be interested in me, as I was 15 years older. I thought he looked on me as a mother.

> Ray was 35 years older than me and I met him when I took up a teaching post at the school where he taught. Though there was no question of a relationship at that time, when he retired at the end of the year I remember thinking what a pity it was that interesting and individual people were leaving the profession, and also that I would never now get to know him better. However, after his retirement I saw him from time to time because we had friends

in common and I gradually got to know him better and visited his house, though it was a long time before the relationship became a sexual one.

The last thing I wanted was to be entangled again so when he wrote to me after we met at my friend's house I really almost didn't respond.

She did respond though and found, like many others, that getting 'entangled' with this particular person helped her to build up confidence in herself.

Restoring Confidence

A number of the people we spoke to were feeling unattractive when they met their age gap partner. They were not getting any recognition from their own age-group, so when attention came from someone quite outside that group – attention from someone quite different – it enabled them in turn to feel different about themselves.

At the time I was really unhappy at work and that was probably why I valued his attention. He would meet me at the station and take me to work and pick me up.

At the time I was under a lot of stress and taking all sorts of drugs because I really felt I had no one to turn to after my marriage failed. Perhaps he was also unsure of how much of his feelings revolved around wanting to help me and companionship.

In these circumstances, the couples valued the ease and intimacy of their relationship – it could be much more fulfilling than any they had had before. Only later they realized that there was more to it than friendship alone.

He was full of jokes and interest and for some months he visited me occasionally and I would go to his flat for lunch. But it was months before it became sexual and I admitted we were not having a friendship but a love affair.

Some actively resisted greater intimacy. Usually the age gap was the most significant reason.

It was simply ridiculous to fall in love with a man old enough to be my father.

I kept thinking to myself, 'I don't want this, it will end in tears. He is young enough to be my son.'

Once embarked upon, if not important before, the age gap became so because it reinforced the relationship. Sometimes the participants realized that they had been ready for this relationship; it was lying in wait for them because of their previous experience. This might be because their own parents had had such a relationship.

My mother was 15 years younger than my father, so I suppose it seemed like a natural pattern.

or for other reasons:

I am now 48 and have always had a penchant for older men. Although I have had just as many relationships with men of about my own age, those in which the man was significantly older than me had, as it were, an added dimension. It's quite simple really. I've always liked having a father-figure; so in these partnerships the normal man–woman relationship was overlaid with a child–parent one. In fact, I was particularly attracted by men who already had children because that seem to add somehow to the 'father' image that I liked to conjure up.

It was a turn-on for me. I suppose, too, I've had quite a few relationships with older men which have been purely child–father in nature. I've been drawn to this kind of thing since adolescence.

Another point I would like to make is that I have always enjoyed a very close relationship with my father, whereas my mother and I haven't always seen eye to eye. I often wonder if I'm looking for a father-figure. Throughout my life I have always got on better with older males, teachers, uncles, work colleagues, etc.

Looking for a mother- or father-figure may be important for some people – a notion we develop in Chapter 8.

Sometimes it was the age difference itself which seemed to make this new scenario more powerful:

The difference in our ages highlighted our intimacy, as if our love against the odds was especially rarefied and intense.

Our circumstance seemed unique. Given all the obvious differences between us in terms of age and experience, it was clear that our love must be different and therefore particularly strong.

The feeling of being in some way odd, seen as strange by the rest of society, was an important element in reinforcing the intimacy for some couples.

One of my reasons for taking an older man was really my desire to be untypical. I had always found the idea of doing what is socially acceptable distasteful.

As soon as people stared, to indicate they thought we were a bit odd, the old 'two against the world' feeling came into operation and made our relationship stronger than ever.

It may be that these people were deliberately seeking that 'two against the world' feeling, actively wishing to be different and expressing that by seeking a partner clearly apart from the norm.

So, do the initial meetings of age gap partners reflect the distinctiveness of their relationships? Our sample of interviewees is insufficiently large to be sure. What we are confident of is that while some met in the same way as any couple, it was a break from the routine or daily pattern that enabled many others to meet or to pursue an inclination or desire they would otherwise have felt they had to pass by. Age gap partnerships may take best root in the distinctive environment of unfamiliar territory.

2

Stages

You mean you can't remember 22 November 1963?

Once established, do age gap couples differ from others? Or do they experience the same combination of smooth sailing with patches of heavy weather that any other relationship does? The answer is a qualified 'Yes' to the latter – qualified, because the basis of compatibility would appear to differ significantly from equal age relationships. Most people choose as their friends, and especially as their partners, people who to a considerable extent share their world-view. That is, they choose people who at a fundamental level share broadly similar values, or beliefs, or opinions. Choosing someone of the same age assists this, in that the chosen partner is likely to have grown up with similar influences, whether from the prevailing social and political processes or simply teenage years exposed to the same music, TV programmes and films.

However, if your partner is someone 15, 20, or even more, years older or younger than yourself, there are going to be some obvious discrepancies in your experiences.

Music is important to me, having grown up in the 1970s and being totally obsessed with music from that period, and that wasn't him at all; that wasn't his field of knowledge. He was into the 1960s and was obsessed with early 1960s music and that posed a problem, and we did eventually just have to play classical music because it was hard to relate to each other on that side. But that whole sort of having grown up in different eras was weird because I just didn't understand . . .

These discrepancies may be serious – some are less so – but you are likely to have to address them either way.

Lack of Shared History

For a start, you do not have a common history. A lack of shared history was commonly reported by our interviewees, and comments such as 'It is odd that he was at work before I was born' or 'I couldn't believe that he couldn't remember where he was when Kennedy was shot' were frequent. When we began our research we wrongly anticipated this might be a major stumbling block.

> When the relationship first began I was surprised how little I was aware of the gap being there. I realized it was conspicuous to others and that we were looked at in the street, and I remember being repeatedly surprised when I had forgotten about it. The obvious things would happen, like talking about Margaret Thatcher being elected and realizing that he was 30 when this happened and I was 14, but this was funny and interesting.
> (woman 27, man 43)

But there are areas of difficulty, as, for example:

> During conversations with his contemporaries which are a discussion of events that happened before I was born but that they have experienced as young adults, then I am acutely aware of the age difference. It feels like a huge, yawning gap. Normally, in everyday life, I am not aware of the age difference.

Alan is a wonderful man and there are times when I adore his friends and love the way they flirt with me in that old-fashioned way, but when we go to some official dinner and they start reminiscing it's pretty dire and I get fed up with telling them I just don't remember Suez or the Lib–Lab pact of the 1970s.

The lack of shared history in itself wasn't quoted as a problem, but some younger partners did resent how it could be used:

One problem I have faced is when my 'youth' is used against me, i.e. they recall events which happened 25 years ago and then say, somewhat condescendingly, 'Oh you weren't even born,' or sometimes they assume that because I'm young, I'm stupid.

Of course, this may be as much about the friends as the age gap! Sometimes it is seen only as a vague annoyance:

The time I feel the generation gap is when the Second World War is mentioned. For me, that is something that happened to my parents and grandparents, but to Jacques it is a very real childhood experience. As a result of this he does have the very annoying habit of hoarding small pieces of soap (as would be found in a hotel room) and he has several large boxes full of it. As one never knows when the next war may be, it is important to have 'provisions of soap' with which to barter!!

But many choose to deal with this humorously:

I boast that I was in the top infants when my first child was born, and had my second one in the top juniors. Such aspects thoroughly amuse me.

As it is frequently the friends of partners who accentuate the lack of shared history (because that may be one of the strongest links the friends have with the partner), the mixing and integrating of these friends sometimes proved unsatisfactory:

> It was simply hopeless when we tried asking our friends to parties or dinners. They just used to stay in separate groups and we'd go back and forth between them trying to get them to mix in some way. We'd each get neurotic that when they slipped back into their age ghettos they were all saying how staid or how silly the others were. So we just stopped it.

> My friends do not like him, they think he has tied me down and that he is boring! He feels the same about them so we usually do things separately. I go out with my friends and he goes out with his; we even go on separate holidays as well.

Some foresee the difficulties ahead:

> I drifted away from my old friends when my marriage broke down (they are all 'our' friends). A side product of having an affair with a married man was that I did not try to make new friends as I never wanted to arrange to meet anyone in case I missed him dropping in. I think the age gap does have an effect in that my old friends would have been too 'young' for Leslie and I am not sure if other people of his age would accept me on such a level.

For others, it is more threatening:

> My partner and I did not have friends in common. This was a problem. He had his own friends and so did I; people all in their twenties. My partner felt threatened if any of these friends were men in their twenties. He put me under pressure to drop them. He did not want to meet them and

the few occasions he did he made it clear he wanted to leave early. As a result I had a social life separately the entire time I was with my partner, and he became very insecure if I went night-clubbing.
(woman 25, man 47)

Frequently the easiest solution was simply to give up trying to integrate the friends. Couples remained friends with one group only, seemingly almost always the older set, and confined their social activities to this group. The younger partner learned to cope:

It was not much of a sacrifice honestly, as her friends were more sophisticated, more worldly, better informed, just a whole lot more interesting, than mine.

I think I felt that he wouldn't be accepted by my friends and I was quite happy to agree with him, 'Yes, my friends are superficial,' so that I didn't have to let the two worlds collide.

An alternative was to find ways of each keeping their own set of friends whom they saw outside the relationship, without trying to integrate both sets.

We've devised ways of dealing with the incompatibility of our two sets of friends. He sees his, I see mine and we each see the others but not together! Then, about once a year, we give a great big bash and they all come to our place but there are so many that you wouldn't notice that the two lots don't mix.

By and large couples seemed to find a lack of shared history an advantage rather than a disadvantage. It brought depth and a different perspective to the relationship which went beyond the introduction to new pursuits. They valued the different views that age gaps could bring: the opportunity to relive or renew experiences previously denied to them. Amongst all the other problems to be resolved in an age gap relationship, that of a lack of shared history did not rate too highly. One respondent did say:

> I do now wonder if it would be nice to share an overlapping frame of reference: popular music, television shows of child and teenhood, fashion, the trappings of ephemeral culture.

But she then went on to give a distinctive opinion of how unimportant the subject ought to be:

> I feel that two people really absorbed in each other are going to transcend that level to a plane of their own universal harmony, to share an intimacy which is not contingent to the specifics of our late twentieth-century urban destiny.
> (younger woman – separated)

Or, put more succinctly,

> If that is the only problem you've got, you are pretty damn lucky!

Different Experiences

If shared history was not particularly significant, then lack of shared experience certainly was.

Whenever two people get together, the life experience each partner has had, and which they bring to the relationship, is one of the cementing factors. Their experiences may match even though they were not actually there to share them with their partner. These provide a comfortable feeling of joint recognition, and this feeling is much more likely if both partners are of an equivalent age, where their values and skills are likely to match.

Contrast this with an age gap relationship. Brought up in the 1980s or 1990s, you are most unlikely not to know how to work a video machine. Someone brought up 20 years before may not have been used even to having a TV set as part of the normal household furniture! Someone brought up in the 1950s or 1960s is likely to have an expectation of a working pattern based upon staying with a single employer. Someone brought up in the 1990s will have an expectation that work where it exists will be based on short term contracts.

Just as significantly, moral values and standards change rapidly. The widespread acceptance of couples living together before marriage was unknown a generation ago, while the issue of women playing an active role in the work-force, having a choice about having children and enjoying equal rights with men, would have been similarly unknown. As we get older we find it harder to keep up with such changes.

But beware: women in their twenties and men in their forties are from different generations, so ideas, ways of doing things are going to be different. Learn together.

I am conscious that Ian is quite a bit older – partly because he is getting increasingly arthritic and deaf, partly because he has some startlingly anachronistic ideas. Like, the eldest son has to arrange the funeral, not the wife! New one to me. And he is much more class-conscious, particularly in terms of village society. I don't mean prejudiced, but aware of the subtle distinctions and ranking that goes on beneath the surface.

These differences of experience are not necessarily a disadvantage. To be at a different stage of life when you meet, and therefore at a different stage of coping with these issues, was often an advantage.

The varying experiences each brings may be one of the key attractions for these partners, along with the new perspectives offered by the relationship. Such perspectives may come from the participants being at different stages of their own life and development. One may have established a career, been through a marriage and had children. The other may only have begun to contemplate them. The older partner can therefore be seen to be bringing knowledge, skills and wisdom to the younger.

> He was incredibly well-read, and I regard myself as being well-read as well, but he had that extra advantage of years where he knew quite a lot of interesting things about writers that maybe it would have taken me a lot longer to get to know. He really had a dramatic impact on my life in the way I see things.

> She makes me feel comfortable and secure because she knows so much and her life has been so rich in experience.

Often this is valued by the younger partner, thus helping to give them confidence and speed up the learning process.

> His experiences are invaluable to me.

Nor should we assume that it is the older partner always who brings the good experience.

> Because he had grown up in a much less restrictive time than I, he was just freer in every way, better at showing his feelings, better at being assertive, much less inhibited in bed, than any man of my own age could possibly have been. This was marvellous for me, of course.
> (an older woman)

However, having once been through a stage of life does not

always mean a partner wants to pass on that experience:

> I thought it would be helpful, him already being the father of two when our first baby was born. I thought he'd be able to help me and give me confidence but it did just the opposite. Whereas he had seen it all before, I felt that made him bored with our baby and, worst of all, I felt he was looking down on me because I didn't know how to do everything perfectly. I really resented the fact that he was not at all at sea, as I was. It would have been so much more unifying if we were learning together.

A sad fact of the human condition is that each person has to learn by their own, not anyone else's, experience. However experienced your partner, there are some things you just have to go through for yourself, otherwise two things happen. Either you don't learn the lesson properly or you feel resentful that the other person has in some way prevented you from going through the growing process which experience some-times, and often painfully, provides.

> Everybody seemed to assume that because Charles was 17 years older I had found the father-figure that I was supposed to have been seeking all those years. They had to be joking! He had an ex-wife and two grown-up children, but if there is a child person in our relationship it certainly is him. He is incapable of taking a decision, of acknowl-edging responsibility, or behaving like a responsible adult. On the other hand, he does act like a parent in one way . . . he is very restricting to me. I literally had to report in when I was out shopping for more than two hours or when I took the kids on a day out, or he would worry about me. But I don't call that acting like a father-figure, I call it being an old woman.

The above interviewee felt her husband restricted her freedom and this can be a problem for the couple at different stages of life. Take the couple who marry when the older husband is near the peak of his career and the wife is just beginning hers. Perhaps she will give up a fledgling career to have children and support the husband who is in need of a stable and secure family from which to pursue his own pressured life. At this point of their lives, and for some time onwards, the differing stages of expectation of career which they are at suits them both extremely well. Yet move on 15 years and we may find a very different scenario. Now retired, the husband, fulfilled and satisfied, wants only a slackening of pace, less pressure, a running down. But what about the younger partner? The children are grown up and off her hands. She begins to be bored, to look for some fulfilment to realize her own potential. She may find a job, become involved in conservation or local politics, or take up some sport or hobby. More time is then spent out of the home, developing a new circle of friends, having people ringing up of whom the husband has never heard. What happens? Unsurprisingly, there is growing resentment from the husband who wants his wife to be at the same winding-down stage of life as he is, not the 'spreading your wings and stepping out' stage.

I think the primary cause of our breakup was the difference in attitude. I was undeniably middle-aged, and set in my ways, whereas Patricia was developing late and on an exponential curve of progress towards the maturity she'd missed out on earlier. As soon as she realized there was a world to be explored, she got itchy feet and wanted to do her own thing, which is understandable. I would certainly warn any prospective age gap partnership about the likelihood of such development. There can be no doubt that the younger partner will usually be more flexible and likely to change his/her mind than the older, despite any other circumstances that may apply.

The older partner might have travelled the world and now

wants only to settle down. Meanwhile the younger is ready to start travelling; which of course does not have to be literal. It may be that the older partner either does not wish to repeat experiences they have already been through, or is simply feeling ready to give up on new experiences.

> He was basically at a different stage in his life to me. But he tried to stagnate the level I was at for his own comfort. This is in hindsight, of course. He wanted a set routine, no holidays abroad and to develop his interest in music and he very much wanted me to sit tight and fit in. One of his favourite phrases was 'You simply don't know about this, you're too young. I do know because I've been there and I've done that.' You have to grow for yourself and in that respect I was not developing because I wasn't allowed to. I became tired of being in the wrong just because of being younger, something I couldn't help but it shouldn't have to be such a disadvantage.
> (younger woman, referring to her husband 17 years older)

Sometimes the age gap itself helped to facilitate the growth of the other:

> Edward has been so constant in his commitment to me; it has offered me a great deal of emotional security, while I have been rushing around Europe trying out different ways of leading a life as an artist. I don't imagine this would have been quite the same had he been as young as me.

The Ageing Process

Much of what we have referred to here as being at different stages of life and the difficulties that can arise is not necessarily about the actual fact of the partners being at different stages. It is about the mental attitudes which they hold as part of those different stages. Being 65 is not what makes you jealous of your wife's outside interests; it is the mental and emotional response which those outside interests invoke in you. So mental age is the most significant aspect, since we had many instances of 60-year-olds who were infants in their heads and 29-year-olds who were extremely mature. It is the emotional maturity or immaturity which is the key factor.

Physical and mental ageing are not only different but they do not run in tandem. There are many youngish people who are mentally old – settled, unwilling for new experiences, minds unwilling to accept challenges or new ideas – and many older people mentally on top of the world and attitudinally much more prepared to be challenged, to take on new activities.

However, there is one aspect of ageing which is not controlled by the mind, or at least only partially. However much you try to ignore it, your body will age. That is an inescapable fact. Women may take hormone replacement therapy and stay fit a great deal longer than their mothers did. Men may exercise and diet to keep in trim. But hair does thin, wrinkles do appear and even with plastic surgery bits start to droop. Our interviewees were conscious of this in themselves . . .

I think the disadvantages for him are happening now. My age is showing, wrinkly upper arms, puffy tummy, horrible jowls and bags under the eyes. I am feeling very bad about this but he swears he sees none of it.

Or, as in the case of Hannah, they were conscious of the effect this had on their relationship:

He frequently hit me and I took it almost in return for his love and in gratitude for him fancying an old bird like me. I was always frightened that Brian would find a younger woman and he would tell me I was ageing, which was so cruel, but his only way of exerting power.

Physical ageing is almost an absolute. Sure you don't know if your older partner is going to have a heart attack or develop Alzheimer's disease, but you do know they will slow down to some extent, will retire, may be concerned about their physical appearance, may not be able to take on the energetic activities of their youth, and that some will definitely have ill health and need to be looked after.

> My older husband is not able to take long walks, garden or match me in physical activity.

Slowing down of sexual activity may be a problem too. What influences a sexual relationship may be largely in the mind but of course reactions are slower, erections not as good, vaginas drier.

> I have to describe the way I gradually and almost imperceptibly became less happy. Our sex life dwindled — not surprisingly given Paul's age, by then nearly 69 — and the fact that he had had a heart attack. Up until then, it had been remarkably satisfying. This decline troubled both of us and created considerable tension in me, over a period of several years. I was increasingly now fairly conscious of the age gap. In the last few years, indeed, before his death, I secretly began to feel trapped. Around the age of 50 I still felt reasonably young and energetic, while Paul, though still lively and young in manner, was unmistakably becoming elderly, a bit more prone to minor health problems, understandably more cautious than he had been; becoming rather set in his ways, I suppose. Outwardly we must still have seemed very close, but I knew this was not the case any more. At times I even felt slightly depressed. I was often rather moody and no doubt difficult to live with at times, but I still loved and admired Paul and hoped

to be a loyal, loving wife for the rest of our time together. If he seemed less warm towards me, I think it was because he was very unhappy too about our sexual difficulties, and didn't know how to cope. We did sometimes try to discuss the topic affectionately, but there seemed no solution. It was something we had to accept. The trouble was that, while I knew this intellectually, it was hard for me to accept in other ways.

There is also worry about the ability to continue a fulfilling sex life:

> After his first heart attack it was downhill all the way because I was certain he'd die in action.

However, many dealt with physical failings phlegmatically:

> I wouldn't change anything in the relationship, but we would both benefit from a new body, were it available.

Caring

> The reduction in NHS provision worries me, since I'd always assumed I'd gets lots of help should it be needed. I'd hate him to become chronically ill or weak. I can't imagine how I'd be expected to look after him myself as he is a physically big man and I could not possibly lift him, etc.

> I may in the future have to decide between caring for my mother or my husband.

Some of the most moving experiences related to us were those where at first the couples had been quite mentally and physically compatible but where, as time went on, the years between them showed in the decreasing physical or mental faculties of one partner. Then the younger one ended up caring for the older in a way which they had never expected. While for some the caring aspect did not occur, for others it was a great fear.

> I have this horrific fantasy about me being an old lady in a wheelchair while he, still young, pushes me along.

Of course there is absolutely no guarantee that even if you are much older than your partner you will be the one to be cared for rather than the one doing the caring. Accidents and unexpected illnesses can occur at any age. But clearly where there is a big age gap, it is more likely that it will be the younger partner who ends up as the carer. This is not always easy to accept:

> Marrying a man 27 years older, I always knew of course there was a possibility I'd be a youngish widow. But I simply never thought I might end up having to care for him when he became an invalid. But that's what's happened. He had a stroke and I didn't become a youngish widow, I became a middle-aged carer, ageing by the day because of the stress of it. We were so happy together I felt running the risk of being a youngish widow was worth it. If you ask me if it was worth it to become an ageing carer, I'm not sure what my answer would be. You don't think about these things enough when you are swept off your feet by a successful older man.

For others, they may accept the inevitable as just one of those unwelcome hands that you get dealt in life.

> You marry for better or for worse; this just happens to be the worse bit.

The key element is that caring for anyone takes place within the context of a relationship and it is the nature, quality and history of that relationship which will determine how stressful the caring role is for both the carer and the cared for. If your pre-caring relationship was one where there was a lot of anger and resentment, and an uneasy balance of power, do not be misguided enough to think that this situation will automatically change if one of you has to care for the other. It won't happen. It would be wise, therefore, to discuss the issue before the situation arises so that each participant knows what they can expect of the other if the need for care arises. We also have some practical advice to give on this in Chapter 9.

Dying and Bereavement

If you have a younger partner, especially if you are an older man with a younger wife or partner, it is highly probable that it will be you to die first. Women who marry men of about the same age can look forward, if that is the right phrase, to about 12 years of widowhood, so the prospect of a prolonged period of widowhood is much stronger for the wife of a much older man. Our interviewees were extremely conscious of this.

> I often used to think about the possibility of him dying, which is something I probably wouldn't have done with a younger partner. This worry was exacerbated by the fact that he smoked and drank so much. He said to me once when he was about 60, 'I've just realized that I probably only have about 10 years of lucidity in front of me.' It was a bit of a shock to me. So the relationship was pervaded by a rather uncomfortable sense of mortality.

> Graham will be due for retirement long before I am and neither of us likes the idea that he will sit at home all day while I work. But we will need to keep getting my salary as we have to bear in mind that I may well spend the last 20

years on my own, so we cannot decide to spend our capital over the estimated remaining years.

In the normal course of events, men tend to die well before their wives. In my case it's possible that I may be without him for a long time. Despite the eating of his greens, he is beginning at 66 to feel a few aches and pains; there are so many things he wants to do and he rages against fate when he is prevented from doing so. He still does not know what he wants to do when he grows up, but dying is certainly not one of them. As a nation I know we are not very good at dealing with the idea of death. When the subject crops up, I do try to explore it with him, as much for my own benefit as for his. In reality, to put it bluntly, emotionally Roy will have a small part to play at the time of his death; I will be left, when I'm least able to, to face the saddest time of my life with all the arrangements and preparations for a life without him. At least having talked to each other, I will have some guidelines within which to act . . . I dread it.

You cannot stop death happening, but you *can* accept that if you are in an age gap relationship the chances of an earlier bereavement are high. Although it is a difficult topic, it is important to discuss it and to plan if possible. This can include financial planning, but 'emotional' planning is equally important. If you are the younger partner, try, for example, to retain enough separate interests so that there will be at least one aspect of your life which you can keep on your own if you are widowed.

I had kept up my membership of the bowls club – though I'd often have preferred to spend my time with Fred at home. When he died I was grateful there was a place I could go where I'd always been on my own. Everywhere else I felt like a spare part.

These are serious issues, which were taken seriously by our interviewees. However, the overall impression given was that lack of shared history, problems about different stages of development and so on could, in a fulfilling relationship, be overcome by good communication, respect and shared laughter.

I've stressed the intellectual aspect, but there's nothing stuffy about it. Mark is a lot of fun and can make me scream with laughter. Spending time with Mark has made me realize that people *don't* grow up – at heart they are always 16, just a little enlightened or embittered. Unfortunately, we live in an ageist society, which tries to suggest anyone over 30 is past it. Society creates these barriers to communication and anyone who crosses them is condemned outright. What matters in this life is finding somebody with integrity, and developing a bond that is based on honesty and mutual respect – they are the *only* criteria which matter; not looks, or wealth, or status, or years.

Clearly, many people pointed out what you may lose on the swings of physical ageing, you gain on the roundabout of greater experience: a wiser view of life.

3

Friends and Family

We have been tremendously happy together, no question. What I think we have done, though, is to retreat slightly more into our own world than we would have done if we had been a more conventional pairing. Our families for example have never been able to cope with it. Janet's parents were always a bit suspicious that I'd married her because she had a bit more money, a house, etc. than my contemporaries. Whereas my mum and dad have never really accepted the fact that we have produced no grandchildren for them because Janet was already over 40 when we married. It may be that we were both seeking a way of keeping ourselves a bit apart from the world and that's why we chose each other in the first place. Anyway, whatever the reason, it has been successful for us if not for others in our families.
(younger man by 17 years)

For most of us 'No man is an island' is true in that we have to live in the context of families and friends and would prefer not to alienate ourselves completely from them. Therefore it is hardly surprising their reactions to our relationships are important. This chapter summarizes the reactions our interviewees reported from friends and families.

Friends

In the previous chapter we suggested that people in age gap relationships found it difficult to integrate their own friends and tended to stick with one group or decided to see them separately. The initial reactions of friends to age gap relationships are outlined below according to the emotions expressed.

Expectation

My friends at university teased me relentlessly before they met him — I think he exploded their preconceptions. I think they were expecting someone like Victor Kiam.

When we came back to England I know I worried what friends were expecting. I don't think my friends here ever commented on the age difference although, because of our unconventional circumstances living abroad, an idiosyncratic relationship of this sort would not have stood out in the way it would have done in, say, Surbiton. Although nothing was ever said, I did feel a bit self-conscious about being with someone who looked so ancient. (He looked older than he really was.)

Several interviewees were anxious about what their friends thought and were sensitive to their reactions. We all like to think our loved ones are loved by people whom we also like, and we may overstate or understate the attributes of our lover in the interests of bolstering their image in the eyes of our friends, or perhaps, of safeguarding them against disappointment.

Incredulity

> But you can't be going out with her; she's old enough to
> be your mother.

> What do you mean, you fancy him? He's old!

If your friends have been used to you seeing a particular type of
person, it may come as a shock when your new partner turns
out to be someone much older or younger, as Vincent's experience shows.

> I could see from the looks on their faces when they met
> her that they couldn't quite believe it. I'd always gone out
> with these girls in jeans who looked a bit scruffy. When
> Louise turned up looking smart and sophisticated I was so
> proud and I could see them thinking, 'What does a
> woman like her see in him?' I also felt a bit ashamed of
> myself, because when I went to pick her up that night and
> saw what she was wearing, I'd almost wished she had been
> wearing jeans because I thought she looked too old as she
> was.

Pessimism

'Well, of course it will never last' is another common response.

> People are so staid in their thinking, aren't they? They
> honestly believe that if anything is a little bit different it
> can't last.

Broadly speaking one's friends and family disapprove and
doubt the validity of gap relationships. The higher up the intellectual scale they occur, the more liberal the attitudes will be.
Of course the older man's male friends will generally

encourage him to 'throw his leg over' and get what he can out of it because it won't go on for very long.

This particular reaction also lends itself to what was described to us as the pop psychology approach. This goes along the lines of

> You are just seeking ... a father-figure ... a daughter substitute ... to recapture your lost youth, etc. etc.

Such reactions may cause anger and resentment in the people who hear it, overhear it, or suspect that their friends are talking about them thus. But any reaction of an outsider to your relationship also says something about the observer. Going against the norm but being happy and contented in so doing can be an uncomfortable challenge to the long-held values of others. Their criticism or snide comments may be as much about their defensiveness as about your relationship, even their jealousy of your good fortune.

Envy

Friends can sometimes react with envy to such a new relationship. Maybe there is a part of them which realizes they may be sidelined if one set of friends is 'ditched'. They may also see that a new older or younger partner offers new experiences which are denied to them:

> To travel business class, which I had never done before, and to walk around the Academia in Venice with someone who actually knew about Canaletto was amazing and I know I rather went over the top when describing it to my friends. Many of them had never been in an art gallery anywhere, let alone in Venice.

Your new relationship may offer a challenge to the more

orthodox style on which your present friendship is based.
Certainly sexual envy is a feature, too:

> I suppose it was fairly obvious from my whole demeanour
> that I was getting laid well and often and, when your
> friends are in a boring marriage or even one which is not
> boring but which is of long standing, then they are bound
> to be a bit envious of all this new and vibrant sex life you
> are having with your younger man.

> When Julie and I first got together after my first wife died, we
> went on this disastrous holiday with these old friends of
> mine. It was on a boat and inevitably in a confined space
> there wasn't a lot of privacy. I know they overheard us
> having sex and it caused tensions because they weren't doing
> it as much and it made them feel inadequate and envious.

Approval

It was not always the case that friends had negative reactions.
Quite the contrary:

> My friends were extremely supportive at the beginning of
> the relationship because they could see how excited I was,
> how important Dean was to me. I was strongly supported
> when I broke off my engagement because of him. When
> the relationship with Dean ended, my friends were very
> angry with him. The age gap was never really an issue for
> anyone.

> The reaction of everybody around me to the relationship
> was, surprisingly, strongly approving. No one so much as
> hinted that 35 years was rather a large gap; instead they
> came out with adages such as, 'Better an old man's darling
> than a young man's slave.'

Occasionally, nothing at all was said.

I have friends who are silent on the subject of our relationship, but when it comes down to it, I value his company more than theirs.

People may profess not to care what their friends think but on the whole it is important to them. Most wanted their friends to accept their new relationship and were relieved when they did, distressed when they did not.

Of course, if pushed, I'd choose her above my friends any day, but I didn't want to do that and it was great when they got to like her, which I knew they would once they knew her, even though she was so much older than all of us.

Families

Although I mentioned him by name to my family I never introduced him to them. This was not so much because of his age but because he looked so outlandish and I thought the two factors together would completely outrage my family. I even gave him money to go out to the pictures on the rare occasions my father came to see me, so they wouldn't meet.

I have never disclosed to my parents that I have been going out and sleeping with men of their own age-group. One reason is that the relationships have never developed into anything long-term. The other is not being sure of their reaction, although both have said that they see me settling down with an older man, but I'm not sure that they are thinking 20 years older. I've broached the subject with 'what ifs' and they haven't been met with 'Don't you dare.'

My mother was appalled at our marriage and it continues to sadden me that she still thinks 'You could have done better'. Age was irrelevant, however. Had he been the right 'sort' then she would have been thrilled.

The reactions of families can be less encouraging than the reactions of friends. Chapter 4 deals with the responses of children and step-children; here we look at the reactions of other family members.

Families and friends differ in the degree to which they try to accommodate partners, as do partners in their attempts to accept their 'other half's' family and friends. With friends, an attitude of 'take it or leave it' can prevail. And where our interviewees found it difficult with some friends, they either dropped them or stopped trying to see, as a couple, those friends who did not accept the relationship. The friends either accepted or rejected the partner, and in many cases *both* partners, very early on.

On the other hand, you have to live with families, and they cannot be dropped or cannot easily drop you. By and large this seemed to be well understood by our interviewees so that, combined with the prolonged exposure that families often had to the new partner, we found frequent comments to the effect that parents 'came round' to the partner, 'got to like them', 'realized how likeable/wonderful/harmless, etc. they were'.

Our families and friends reacted with extreme caution about the vulnerability of falling in love at our age! And subsequently, with delight when they got to know him or me, as the case might be, and realized it was going to work. My children were very supportive during a transition which was painful for them (I moved to the country to

join him). His children, being much older and more detached, didn't express much opinion.
(woman 43, man 60)

Not all families can be persuaded, though:

Our friends are very supportive and so are his family. My family are of a different kind. They are the type who assume that the benefits are stacked in the older man's favour and I am just playing with his money. I have attempted most aspects to get them to see a reasonable point of view including Relate and The Samaritans after a particularly cutting telephone call from my father concerning deformed children. I have been told that time is a healer but the only time my parents will allow for is the time that Gerry is no longer around. I am, however, lucky that Gerry and I can discuss it and that he is knowledgeable enough to realize that it is not personal (mainly because my parents have only met him once!).

The reactions of families, like those of friends, can also be grouped by their emotional responses to the relationship.

Horror and Revulsion

These are strong words, but the reactions of families can be exceedingly strong:

I have a daughter only one year older than him and a son four years younger. They took the view that if Angelo made me happy it was OK. His family was a different story. Quite awful. He'd had other older women and at first they looked on me as more of a sexual experience. They even lent us a house to meet in. But when they knew it was more serious, they told him I was past my sell-by date and he should move on. They had all kinds of schemes to break us up, and by the time of our marriage, were openly hostile. They asked us not to marry, then forbade us, asked us to postpone. They were ill, we'd cause them heart attacks or even death. All the family rang us and there were threats of suicide. They even planned to kidnap him as a last ditch before the wedding. They have lost him for ever, as he has never spoken to them again. They have sent poison pen letters and turned his whole family against him. Perhaps it is because they wanted grandchildren but the depth of their disgust is quite frightening. They say it is obscene, abnormal. I find it profoundly threatening.

The revulsion sometimes centred around the physical side of the relationship, and may well have its roots in the sexual taboos which forbid incest.

Somehow the thought of an old man like him touching me was terrible to my parents.

This, of course, may be encouraged by some couples. One man openly admitted that he realized part of the attraction of his young wife for him was precisely because there were elements of incest, which they both found exciting.

Disappointment

Many families expressed great disappointment with the match. This can be because they had held an image of the kind of person their offspring would fall in love with and the 'chosen one' was definitely not it.

We always thought our daughter would marry a young chap who could be like another son to us but she turned

up with this almost elderly chap who was pretty well our age and it just didn't seem right.
(from a mother)

It was also often to do with the realization that the match would be unlikely to produce children.

Directly he introduced me to her and I saw that she was so much older then I realized I'd be unlikely to have grandchildren. Then when I found she already had two children who were pretty grown-up, it made me even more sure. When I knew her better and found she'd been sterilized after the birth of her second, I heard the door finally shut on my hopes of grandmotherhood.

I quite liked him but you could see he wasn't the sort of man who would want his ordered life disturbed by children. He had everything planned and these plans were not going to be upset by kids, so I've had to come to terms with that.

In addition, some prospective grandparents expressed disappointment that their new daughter- or son-in-law was already experienced as a parent, thus depriving them of the opportunity to act as an advisor or guru (or interfering old bag or codger!) when the kids came along. Others took pleasure in finding themselves with a ready-made set of grandchildren, but for most the feeling that 'It's not the same as having your own' prevailed.

Fear

Families reacted fearfully largely because they wanted the best for their relatives. They were worried that an age gap relationship would be more difficult to maintain when everyone knows that any marriage is difficult enough. The rising divorce rate and all the other examples they see around them strike panic into the hearts of families who fear unhappiness for their offspring. Anything which puts more stress on a relationship, or was seen as potentially doing so, was understandably resisted by families.

> My mother was not in the least bit concerned about the age gap, so she said. All that she was concerned about was that I should be happy and I could not be with someone so much older. The reactions of my partner's family were not as bad. His mother accepted me, albeit a bit reluctantly . . .

> Our wedding was a family occasion, at which my grandmother made a scene because of her disapproval of the age gap. She felt that I would be sure to be abandoned by him because he was younger.

Guilt

> My mother's reaction was to ask where she went wrong. She clearly felt that somehow she had failed in her upbringing of me that I should choose a partner so far from the norm.

It is understandable that parents should feel this. Most parents set out on parenthood with some kind of notion that they are going to be perfect parents, or at least to be a great deal better than they felt their parents were to them, but it is a lucky parent who ends up still feeling this by the time their children become teenagers! Parents are extremely susceptible to feelings of guilt. Somehow, whatever you do, you should always have done it better or differently. While we all probably have an image of the ideal match we hope our children will make, it would be a rare parent whose ideal match for their offspring was someone much older or younger than their child. A mother may fantasize that she wants her daughter to marry someone who will look after her or, similarly, that her son will find someone who will be a steadying influence. Let the offspring then bring home a man the same age as mother is, or worse, a woman old enough to be a mother to the precious son, and she may feel little differently!

Sometimes a parent's guilt has its roots elsewhere. When Phyllis found out that her son was gay, she was consumed with guilt. All she could think of was, 'Where have I gone wrong? How have I failed as a mother?' Because her son's partner was much older, she decided to see him as the focus of blame.

> I realize it was only to try to absolve myself from the guilt, but I was convinced that Danny had been led astray by Neil and that he would never have gone down that route if it hadn't been that a much older man had in some way corrupted him. It is a good job that I eventually got out of that way of thinking because, years later, Danny himself took up with Jamie who was very much younger than him. I'd have had a job seeing my own son as a corrupter, wouldn't I?

Support

Despite the stories of family opposition, it is not inevitable that parents will oppose the age gap relationships of their offspring. For many families, love for the son or daughter naturally encompassed support for the partner of their choice:

> My parents approved of the relationship because they liked Jon (who was in fact older than them). They were just a little worried that if we married and had children I might be left to bring them up on my own.

The reaction of families to age gap relationships will in part depend on the pattern of loving relationships within the family. If your own parents had a big age gap between them and have been happy together, they are going to be more tolerant and accepting of their children's relationships. What we have to understand is that there are potentially more difficulties for parents when coming to terms with these partnerships than with 'ordinary' relationships.

Confusion

What is different about age gap relationships is that they break the common pattern of lovers and parents: the expectation that you and your lover will belong to one generation, and your parents to another. With an age gap relationship, this may not be so clearly defined, and confusion may ensue. Consider Raymond's experience:

I'd been going out with Imogen for several months and had started to bring her name into every conversation, like you do when you are in love. I obviously did it with my mother, too, but I did resist introducing them in a way that was quite different from my other girlfriends. It is difficult to decide whether I didn't want to introduce her to Mum because Imogen is only three years younger than she is or because somehow I knew that she was *the one*, the person I was going to end up with, I mean. Anyway, of course eventually I had to do it but I never warned Mum about the age difference. I suppose I thought she had sussed it out because I used to talk about Imogen's children who were quite grown up. They were both a bit wary at first but a bit competitive. I think that is quite usual though, when potential mothers and daughters-in-law meet. It is something about 'I know him better than you do', I think. They obviously liked each other though and warmed to each other. What I wasn't prepared for was just how excluded I'd feel when they started to talk about things I didn't remember. It was me who felt out of it. For a while it was really a problem because when we went to stay at my mother's, you know how you always feel a bit as though you are a small boy again at your mum's house? Well, I had two of them making me feel like that. We've worked it out now, but there were some sticky moments.

The roles that people expect to play have been confused; they are not sure who or where their alliances lie. Raymond didn't know whether he was in alliance with his partner or in opposition to the affinity shared by Imogen and his mother. This confusion can lead to a few awkward situations.

How the World Sees You

Reaction from friends and family was not the only feedback couples received on their relationship. Because of their visual distinction, many couples could also intimate how society in general viewed them.

I remember when we were first invited to dinner with two of Brendan's friends, a couple in their forties, that afterwards the man was supposed to have said that I was nice but 'a bit young', which sounded so odd, as we couldn't think for *what* I was a bit young.

Of course people always look amazed when they hear that I have a partner 25 years senior, and they usually say something like, 'Oh, but I expect he looks much younger than he is', and I have to say, 'No, he looks every bit 53.'

Many developed an appropriate response:

An obvious disadvantage is that people quickly spot an age difference of 20 years and feel quite entitled to openly stare. I felt we stuck out as an 'office affair' and resented the tag – clever older man/stupid younger woman, or rich egotistic older man/scheming younger woman. As our relationship lasted year after year I found myself making a point of saying things like 'We went to such and such place three years ago' in conversation with outsiders so they would know that it was a long relationship.

Others relish the obvious confusion:

I do sometimes quite enjoy the fact that people can't always work out our family when out together due to all the different ages splitting all the generations. My husband is actually nearer my mother's age than mine and my grandmother is nearer my father's age than my mother's. Then my brother's girlfriend is nearer my husband's age, while my brother and I are nearer my husband's children's ages!

For some couples, to be perceived differently, stared at or pointed out may bind them together more closely – united against the world.

I hate being mistaken for his daughter. It has only happened rarely and it was mortifying for both of us. The most embarrassing time was when we were on holiday in New Zealand and we checked into a small town hotel and they gave us two single rooms! Having to face that kind of situation sure develops bonds between you.

Of course, you're always going to meet with some hostility when in age gap relationships. I've had people say to me, 'But what can you possibly have in common?' to which I reply 'Everything!' Why can't people be happy for us? I think it's only because our differences are visible that people feel free to pass judgement. There are plenty of couples from far less likely matches than ours who are tolerated because they look the part. I know for a fact that people assume I'm a gold-digger or that he is a dirty old man but that's their problem – I certainly don't want to waste my time reassuring people. If anything, these detractors just draw us closer together and make us aware that our relationship is special somehow. You don't get many chances at happiness – you should take them when they come along and not try to please other people.

Although successful relationships are about sharing, commitment and communication, there are those partnerships which need excitement and stimulation in order to succeed. We all know successful relationships where both partners row frequently, but where such arguments have an essential functional role in satisfying the needs of each partner and in maintaining the relationship. For some partners in age gap relationships, the stimulation afforded by external comment and internal differences may be essential for their personal needs within the relationship.

We were living together for six months and didn't tell anyone . . . it was so exciting.

It may be that the external reactions from friends, family and the world is exactly what some age gap couples are seeking. It may fulfil some need for attention. Being seen as a rebel couple, two against the world, is another reason for going into the relationship in the first place.

The reactions and approval of friends and families are important to any couple, and age gap couples are no different in this respect. What may differ for them is that the initial reactions of friends and families will focus on the obvious age difference and it will take longer for their judgements to be based more on the characters of each of the couple. Although there will remain those who are wary or opposed to an age gap partnership *per se*, many will react just as they would to a more conventional partnership.

4

Babies and Children

In an age gap relationship, having children does not appear to be as likely, nor does it seem to play such a central part, as it does in a same age relationship. Certainly children did not feature centrally for many of those we interviewed. However, there do seem to be three significant aspects to consider with regard to age gap relationships and children. These are:

- having no children at all
- having children at a late stage of life for one of the partners
- having step-children when you are almost the same age as the offspring of your partner

No Children

An age gap couple may deliberately choose not to have children or they do not have children for practical reasons. Clearly, one such reason may be the age of the older partner:

Children was never an issue, for the simple reason that I was already past the menopause when we met. I think I was careful to tell him that on our second date so he would not harbour any hopes!

We have kept economic independence and maintained separate identities and lifestyles alongside each other.

However, children change everything and should not be brought into the world unless you are prepared to help them and put your own needs second if necessary.
(from a couple who chose not to have children)

The most likely reason for choosing not to have children is that the older partner does not want a second family and to have to go through raising children again:

One of my jokes in the early years was to say, 'Fancy, if I'd been a Catholic, we would have had four children by now.' He certainly could not have survived being a parent again, and everyone's life would have been a misery.

I had to accept that if I married him there would be no children. He didn't exactly say so, but he already had four and they were very grown-up. It was not as difficult to decide as you might imagine, because what we had together was so good it was worth any sacrifice. He was the first man I had ever been involved with who didn't mangle me emotionally and I worshipped him for it; still do actually. The other side of the coin is that in fact I must be the sort of person to whom children are not of vital importance, otherwise I'd never had fallen for Derek, would I?

Partners may well choose not to have children because they recognize they would have opposing views on how to bring them up. Different generations have differing standards of expectation as to the behaviour and upbringing of children. Ideas about child rearing change rapidly and are quickly absorbed into our minds. If you yourself were brought up under the Truby King discipline of rigid time schedules and strict rules, you will find it hard that your younger partner has absorbed a culture of Penelope Leach which advocates that 'baby always knows best'.

When we married he said I could have a child if I wanted, but fortunately I said I preferred our partnership, since I quickly realized that our value systems bore no relationship and I would have totally disapproved of his way of bringing up our children. He gets irritable and moody and that would have upset me to see my child nagged at, so I'm sure we would soon have separated.

Similarly, if your own teenage was one in which you were expected to be seen and not heard, to give up your seat to a lady and ask before you took a biscuit from the tin, you may not take too kindly to having offspring who expect to dominate the conversation, scarcely move their feet from the sofa to allow you to sit down, and 'graze' when they feel like it.

Her kids just seemed so undisciplined, and I couldn't stand the noise and what I thought were sheer bad manners.

Our interviewees spoke thoughtfully about the choices they had made in having to decide between either children or the partner.

The greatest loss was something which never came about but which I anticipated and worried about a great deal. Whenever I was thinking about a serious future for us it troubled me very much that if we had children together, Ian would be an older father. I am the child of older parents, both of whom had died by the time I was 26. Their illnesses and deaths were very harrowing. When I told someone about my worries, she seemed shocked I could think this way and said that anything could happen in any relationship and that it was finding the right person that mattered; but I think that for her the situation was imaginary, whereas I've seen the real thing and I know how awful it is. I always said I would never create the situation for anyone else ... My feelings for Ian overrode everything else, but it would always have been a shadow over the relationship had we had children.

I do not think I would want to embark on a relationship now with a much older man as I would like to have children and would – to put it bluntly – want to have a viable father. I think if you decide to have a family, the contingent, as opposed to the absolute, factors in the relationship come to the foreground. If the contingent factors contain a lot of diversity, however creative this has seemed in terms of an exciting passion, the very practical task of bringing up children could be made a lot more difficult than it purportedly already is.

Some age gap couples were very practical about the potential problems:

I have three adult children but my partner has no children and we do not intend to have a family, even if it is possible. I mention this because one obvious area of problems, i.e. children, which has to be considered in a gap relationship will not occur in our case. It does mean, however, that we face a period of life very much driven in on ourselves, and we have tried to consider the down potential of the age difference from that standpoint. (woman 39, man 59)

From the many conversations we have had and correspondence received from age gap couples, we also wonder if another reason they do not go in for children is because of the nature of the relationship itself.

First, they are drawn to someone who is older or younger precisely because they do not want to have children and the relationship gives them an excuse for not doing so. Until recently it has been relatively unacceptable in our society to say you do not want children. The concept of 'child-free' rather than 'childless' is a new one. With the publicity constantly given to those who attempt to move heaven and earth – go through pain and huge inconvenience, not to mention expense – in order to have children, it may not be easy for people to admit their feelings. But an age gap relationship provides the perfect excuse.

> We have no children. I never wanted any because I wanted independence and always felt from a very early age that I might behave to my children as my parents had behaved to me, and I could never live with the guilt of doing that. My husband had been married for 25 years and had a daughter some four years older than me, so he himself was not childless.

Sometimes the feelings are so unacceptable that even the couple don't admit it to themselves:

> We thought about it at first and I had two miscarriages. I'm not good with children in spite of having two by my first marriage. I don't think they do a lot for a relation-ship. I thought he wanted them but it turned out I was wrong. He thought I did and we both worked to the wrong assumption. We have lots of loving and nurturing to do to each other. The things we value are our uninter-rupted time together, our leisure; call it selfish if you like.
> (older woman)

> I remember my mother always used to tell me that I was too selfish and self-centred to have children and I was very hurt by this. But I realize she had a point and that one of the reasons that I have teamed up with an older woman is because it provides the perfect excuse for me not to have kids, while not having to own up to being selfish and wanting all the attention for myself.
> (younger man)

Second, the relationship is so fulfilling in itself that children would be superfluous or simply get in the way.

> We are turned in on ourselves, no question. I suppose some would say selfish and they might be right. We choose to spend our time together indulging each other, not children. That is our choice and we have not regretted it.

Several interviewees expressed very strongly that the relationship with their partner was so intense that they had no time for anything else. Many age gap couples seemed to have a better level of communication, a greater level of understanding than did many other types of relationship and it may be that this either took up all the emotional space in the relationship or that the participants were more naturally wrapped up in each other or themselves so as to leave neither time nor space for children.

A third possible reason is that those within age gap relationships may be fulfilling their parent–child roles within the relationship itself. They therefore don't seek anything extra in the way of parenting. They are gaining more fulfilment of the parental role within their loving relationship than would normally be expected and therefore do not need to seek the extra fulfilment they might gain from being an actual parent.

People may also seek different kinds of fulfilment in age gap relationships than they would in equal age ones and therefore children are not so likely. For example, the participants in our survey talked about remaining single within the age gap relationship:

> We each married for friendship and companionship and that has been totally fulfilled. In many respects we are like two single people sharing the same house since we continue to have our independent lifestyles.

Economic independence is important so one can maintain a separate identity and lifestyle alongside that of the partner, i.e. be more like a single. However, children change everything and should not be brought into the world unless you are prepared to help them and put your own needs second if necessary.

In many cases people go into age gap relationships for purely 'adult' reasons i.e. for companionship, ideas, stimulation or bolstering of ego. Children would possibly intrude on this.

Yes, I have missed out on being a father but what I've had makes up for it and, incidentally, I am looking forward to being a grandfather by proxy without the pain of the sleepless nights!
(younger man)

Most of our interviewees were only too well aware of the stresses and strains which children create within a relationship, and acknowledged these as readily as they did the joys to be achieved in parenthood. Some were already making considerable compromises in the relationship simply because of the age gap itself. They knew the limits of their ability to compromise and chose to stay childless. This was helped when the relationship was very fulfilling. If it was all-consuming and had no space for kids, they were grateful that it was so strong. They chose to safeguard that.

Later Children

Despite a certain amount of initial hesitation, many age gap couples do decide to have children.

Right from the start he was adamant that he didn't want to get married and have children. I am passionate about having children. We know of three other couples who are in the same boat. The woman feels a strong biological need whereas the man seldom does. After three years I obviously have persuaded him that I won't be running off with a younger man and we have decided that not having children will be something we'll regret. So far I have changed his life. All credit must go to him for moving because I couldn't live in his poky place. He has given up the financial security of old age and of just beginning to be irresponsible again.

Where a couple in an age gap relationship decide to have children, the previous experience of the older partner can be a great asset – if they choose to see it that way. But the children will have come late to one of the partners and may come at a price, as a group of people interviewed by the *Independent* made abundantly clear:

> As you get older, doctors tell you not to lift heavy things but get real. How do you deal with your toddler? I know many older parents suffer back strain and torn ligaments and sometimes with one partner more enthusiastic than the other.

We all know, from the examples of Charlie Chaplin and Picasso, that men can father children until well into old age. What we should bear in mind is that neither Chaplin nor Picasso necessarily had anything to do with the physical rearing of the babies. They may have walked the floor with them at night but it seems rather unlikely!

Of course there are risks, too – particularly for an older mother – of birth complications or defects such as Down's syndrome, which have to be borne in mind. In addition, there is the risk of being left as a widow or widower to bring up the child alone because the older partner is more likely to die while the child is still young.

It may not be only physical changes which make child bearing and rearing more demanding for older partners, but also psychological factors. The physical and mental wear and tear of children is more difficult the older you get:

Here is what other older parents interviewed for the *Independent* said:

Hangovers are the worst. I used to be able to enjoy a night on the tiles and function fine the next day at work after two hours sleep and a couple of paracetamols. Now it is just not worth it. The kids are merciless and my body's just not up to it. It can take me days to recover; meantime I'm too ill to look after them and they are a danger to be with when my defences are down. Having children in your forties means you pay a physical price.

Recovery time is longer and you can't just relax. On Sunday instead of a leisurely breakfast and read and Radio 3 you find yourself watching *Postman Pat* and throwing the papers away three weeks later, unread.

We just don't answer the phone after 9 p.m. Friends our age without kids just don't get it – but we are too tired to be coherent.

Where the older partner has experience of children, if this experience isn't used to support the younger one, it may create insecurity and difficulties for them too.

However hard I tried to catch up I always felt at a disadvantage as a parent because the simple fact was that he had been through it all before. So when the baby had colic or needed to be toilet-trained it was always something he had experienced with his older children whereas it was first time for me. It made me very insecure and pretty incompetent, I think; or at least that is what I felt.

Step-children

From Cinderella onwards, step-families have been seen to be a problem. In this book, we cannot provide an analysis of step-parenting or give definitive advice, but we can point out the things which are distinctive about being a step-parent when you are nearer the age of the child than that of your partner.

> I am like a big sister to his two daughters and used them as a confidante to compare notes in the early days (though they had left home by time of marriage). And I think they were all glad he'd found another companion after 15 years. When we announced our engagement, the older daughter (aged 23) said, 'Thank goodness someone else can look after him,' as she believed having a widowed father was likely to impinge on her freedom.

There are strong links here with the difficulties associated with caring for an ageing relative which we referred to in Chapter 2. Some children may find it a relief to have a substitute carer come on to the scene, at least if they are sufficiently grown up to have faced, and been frightened by, the issue.

In other circumstances, where a step-parent is much younger, this can be a source of shame and embarrassment.

> I think the worst thing for Joanne was not so much that I remarried but that I remarried someone who was younger than me. She never said so but I am convinced that the reason she was so uptight about it was that it somehow made it more obvious that we were doing it, and you know how horrified teenagers usually feel about their parents' sex lives. She just would never bring her friends home after our marriage and it caused a terrible rift between us.

The fact the age gap between my children and my husband was a lot less than between us caused a lot of problems, particularly with my daughter, now aged 21, at the beginning.
(married when she was 37, he was 20)

Step-parenting, while being one of the most difficult of all relationships, may present extra problems if you are either very near in age to the child, or so much older that you are more like a grandfather than a father. Lucille married a man who was old enough to be her son's grandfather when her children were 14 and 15:

> I can't tell you how awful it was being pig in the middle, in fact I suffered from ulcerating colitis because of it. My tension was so great it came out physically. The real problem was that, because he was so much older, his own experience of parenting was too far behind him and he couldn't remember what it was like. Anyway, in his age-group I think his wife probably did it all. He just couldn't come to terms with my more laid-back style of parenting and the fights between him and the boys were dreadful. So much so that Martin left home when he was barely 17 and didn't return until after Henry died suddenly a few years later.

For the younger partner, another difficulty is being expected to understand the rules of parenting and behave as a parent when you have no experience of being one and when you are not much older than the child. Acting as a parent is not easy if you have absolutely no experience of being one.

> Catherine could never understand my relationship with my son and thought I was being hopelessly indulgent to him. I suppose she'll only know when she has her own kids.

It could be that, within a family situation, with all its pressures and expectations it is difficult to remember that you are not the step-child's parent and should not expect yourself to act like one. If you do, you will set up all the problems which Stuart found:

> Her two girls were teenagers when we got together and there I was in my late twenties, with absolutely no experience setting myself up as their father. In fact I had less than no experience because as an only child I had not even had a sister in her teens to see. I somehow thought that I owed it to Alice to father her girls, as their own father took very little interest. Of course I was completely hopeless at it and they gave me a very hard time. I then felt a failure, Alice felt like piggy in the middle and let down by me and there were some terrible scenes. In fact I have to say it nearly broke us up. But then we went to a step-parents' group and saw a counsellor and gradually came to see what was happening. In the view of the girls I was like a usurper on two counts. I had come in, little older than them and taken a lot of their mother's attention away. Not only that, I'd tried to replace a father and, as they thought, that meant their own father stayed away. The only way to deal with it was to be more detached, leave the mothering to Alice and the fathering to their own father. I did that and thank God it worked and their own father is much more involved again now.

A few of our couples met after the death of the older partner's spouse. Their subsequent remarriage to a younger wife in a couple of cases created enormous hostility from the man's teenage children. On the basis of these comparatively few cases of remarrying after the death of spouse, it would appear essential to take into consideration the feelings of the children. Their grieving and loss will contribute to their hostility towards the new partner, who is then seen as an intruder.

But we don't want to be all doom and gloom about step-parenting across the years. There are times when both partners and children see the fact that the ages are near as a positive advantage. It can sometimes help, as in Petra's case:

> My daughter was not the easiest of teenagers and I had a hard time when my husband left me, especially when I started to bring other men home, even though I was very careful and, I hope, sensitive about it. Nonetheless it was simply hopeless if she saw the man in any way as a potential step-father. She would make their life and consequently mine absolute hell. When Adrian came along, though, it was entirely different and I am sure that was because he was so much younger that he could not possibly be seen as a normal step-father type. In addition, because he had never had any children of his own he did not attempt to act like a father-figure; more like a brother or friend, I suppose, and therefore it was all OK.

or Margaret's:

> His children bridge the age gap between me and mine. Also jealousy is minimal because of the split generation between everyone. His children have left home creating more space emotionally and physically, but they remain in close contact with us and their mother (with whom I'm on good terms). We haven't had the problems of different sets of children under the same roof. There is no feeling of me being a wicked step-mother; I'm more like a big sister to his children, as they are to mine.

Since less than 12 per cent of all age gap marriages in the UK are first marriages for both partners, it is extremely likely that a high proportion of age gap marriages (and cohabitations) will have involvement with children from previous relationships. Don't assume it will be all plain sailing. It may seem so at first.

It is common to ask a newly formed couple, 'How do you get on with his/her children?' and receive the reply, 'Oh marvellous, they are so pleased to have a new mother/father.' Don't believe a word of it! We strongly recommend talking to others in similar situations and getting in touch with an agency, such as The Step Families Association, which can provide you with solid and sensible advice.

But don't be frightened off, either. Think of the advantages. As Michelle said,

> The gains are that I inherited four children and subsequently seven grandchildren. I have an extremely good relationship with all my step-children; the daughters are very close to me. The losses are, I suppose, not having children of my own but I decided once we started living together that having children of my own would be out of the question and very unfair on the children of my partner's first marriage and on my partner. My partner was quite willing for me to have a family if I so wished. With hindsight I'm am very glad I made that decision as it became obvious when my elder step-daughter and her children came to live with us that children of our own would have destroyed our relationship.

and Joan:

> I am now a step-great-grandmother (and was a grandmother the day we married) and I love advocating, 'Have your family my way — by proxy: no fuss, no expense, no worry. The perfect solution.' I truly believe this: I love to have lots of relatives, without the inconvenience.

Just think: you might get to be a grandmother or step-grandmother without ever having to give birth!!

5

Sex

Here's Alice about her older partner:

> Older men have already explored their own sexuality so it gives you the freedom to discover yours. With your peers it's all groping and fumbling and they didn't know what the **** they were doing. Older men take pleasure in introducing you to new experiences; they make you much more aware of your own sexuality and you feel more powerful.

and James about his:

> It was so marvellous to make love to a woman who knew what she wanted in bed but wasn't too demanding. Some women of my age are inclined to give too many directions nowadays and I find that off-putting.

People find it hard to talk about their sexuality. Even in these liberal times it is difficult to be entirely open and honest about our sex lives. Yet there are few people who are indifferent to sex or to the effect of sex in their personal relationships. For many couples it can be either the mortar which holds them together or the wedge which drives them apart. We wanted to know whether there was anything different or special about the age gap couples when it came to their sex lives together; anything which applied to these couples in particular which was not found in other couples where the age gap was smaller. Though sometimes reluctant to start, once warmed up on this subject it was difficult to stop our interviewees – seemingly rather like some of their sexual encounters!

Three areas were of special significance for these couples. This is not to say they are unimportant to other couples, only that they are likely to be more significant in an age gap relationship. These are:

- different levels of experience
- different levels of desire
- different sexual manners

A fourth area that one might expect to figure prominently, that of differing physical characteristics, especially those to do with the ageing of the body, was apparently not of great importance, except to a few older partners who were concerned for their partners about the effects of ageing on their own bodies.

Almost all our interviewees were couples who had been seeking a marriage-type partner and had either successfully established such a relationship or had been trying to achieve one in their previous shorter-term age gap relationships. But we are well aware that there are some age gap relationships which appear to be more strongly centred around sex and where a long-term committed relationship is not in either partner's mind. These are those affairs beloved of the popular press: the older rich businessman with the attractive young woman (Halpern/Wright, etc.), where the man remains married or leaves his established partner, or, increasingly, the successful established woman takes up with the younger male hunk, a pattern which seems to be becoming familiar in the US. We have given these primarily shorter-term age gap relationships a chapter of their own (*see Chapter 6*), but we also refer to them here because sex is a major component of such affairs.

If sex is the mortar that binds relationships, it also plays more than one role. As sex therapies make clear, the loading of other meanings and functions on to the physical activity can create problems where sex becomes the surrogate for something else, or becomes a symptom of something else which is wrong within the relationship. An older man may embark on an affair with a younger woman at a time of life when he fears his potency is in decline. The affair therefore does two things. By providing a new partner it boosts his desire but it also proves to the outside world that he is potent, thus increasing his confidence in himself and therefore boosting his sexual power yet further! Used as a cure for waning potency this can have its problems, as Katrina's experience shows.

When Ralph and I met, he was having problems in his first marriage but also recovering from an affair with a model who had really undermined his confidence by telling him he wasn't as good in bed as any of her previous lovers. He was in fact virtually unable to get an erection at all. I was young enough for him to be flattered by my attention but not so young as the model, therefore not so threatening. Also I had had enough inadequate lovers by this time to know how to deal with it all. I literally gave him all the sexual attention in our relationship for about two years solid. We married and it continued to get better. But somehow he was always afraid that he would lose it again and so he was a bit frantic about it all ... He always wanted to take every opportunity possible to make love, and it was never relaxed. I was worried, too, I suppose, that some time the old impotence would return. There were so many times when he would wake me up first thing in the morning to have sex, when all I wanted was to grab a bit more shut-eye. But always the fear hung over us both of 'use it or lose it'. Of course you'll know what is coming. Yes, of course, he traded me in for a younger model who he said made him feel more confident in bed!

Men do feel anxious as they grow older about their waning powers and, if their partner is much younger, it is likely to make it worse, as Jerry found:

What I would change about my own relationship is indeed the gap, at least to a maximum of 10 years. Whilst sexuality clearly varies at any age among one's fellow men, nevertheless it will probably fade by comparison with a younger female partner and although I do not suggest that this is the only component of love it is a very important aspect as an expression of affection in most relationships.

Because people find it difficult to talk frankly about their sexual difficulties, men like Ralph and Jerry above would not always be so open. They might accuse their wives of not paying them enough attention or of spending too much time with the children when what they really mean is, 'You don't make the sex exciting enough.'

Similarly, women may tell their husbands that they are mean with money or not sufficiently generous with the household expenses when what they *really* want to say is, 'You are not good enough in bed.'

Sex can be a substitute for lots of things. It can be a way for people to prove their worth to their partner. They can exercise power through it:

The sex was the one area of our relationship where I really felt I had some kind of control.

It can also be a means of communication, and may be all these things at the same time, as well as separately. What it rarely is, though, is simple. People's ideas, repressions and hang-ups about sex are started early in life and continue to plague most of us for ever. The relationship in which partners are completely open about their sexual feelings is a rare one. And what you can be sure of, at least in a continuing sexual relationship is that, the better the communication, the better the sex. Because age gap couples seem to make more effort to communicate than others, they are likely to have good sex lives so long as the age difference itself does not pose a problem due to health worries.

> Sex was always quite light-hearted to take the pressure off, but sometimes it would still be a disaster. At the back of my mind was the thought that he'd die on the job. It was my first fear, having raised his heart rate, and so my attention became focused on him, and I worried if I'd get anything out of it. Jack had had two angina attacks, so there was some concern. I found myself being more proactive and I always ended up on top because he hadn't the energy. That's a classic, isn't it?

Let's look at the three most common potential difficulties for age gap couples: different levels of experience and different levels of desire, and different sexual manners.

Different Levels of Experience

Sexual experience is not just about the *amount* of experience people have but also what type of experience they have enjoyed. For many, it is the stage of sexual development people are at when they meet that is the turn-on, and our interviewees certainly valued this:

> Our passion gained much of its energy from our differ-ences — they highlighted our intimacy.
> (younger woman)

> She did teach me to be a considerate lover and made up for my lack of sex education and training!
> (younger man)

I've been with men of my own age and conclude that older men are more accomplished sexually – they are less concerned about their own orgasm and more concerned with achieving mutual pleasure. Older men screw for longer and tend to know your erogenous zones instinctively. Of course I generalize, but I find young men often think a woman's body is just breasts and vagina. Because of his experience, Edward is a really wonderful lover.

We went away to Italy for a week when we had known each other three months. We had sex everywhere, in posh hotels, small pensiones, in fields and in the sea. She was so much more adventurous than any woman I'd ever had before and it was so exciting. We only had to drive past a field of corn for me to know that we would both be thinking the same thing – could we stop and have sex there?
(man 13 years younger)

If age gap relationships offer a freedom from the tramlines of peer pressure and expectation to conform, this may be doubled in spades for sex. You probably read the phrase 'liberal times' in the first paragraph without query, and yet, although much of a titillating nature can be written about sex in the press or talked about on TV, we are not especially liberal in our attitudes to sex. What people think in private may be very different from what they express in public. One consequence of this is that there is often a disparity between the popular image of a society endlessly having it away every which way, and the individuals who not only know this is far from their own personal experience but are nervous and fearful about expectations of them in the bedroom. For many, a much older or younger partner releases them from such pressures to perform and behave 'correctly'. Freed from such burdens of expectation, the sex proves to be remarkably successful.

Several younger men did say that they had been finding that

young women of their own age were very prescriptive about what they wanted in bed. 'It was a bit like doing it by numbers,' said one. Thus, one of the things they appreciated in their relationship with an older woman was the generosity they showed as well as the fact they were more relaxed in bed.

We both agreed that it was nice to sleep with somebody who was not an enemy, and to whom lovemaking meant what the word says.

It is not necessarily the older partner who has greater experience or confidence. Often, the reverse of that expectation can be part of the attraction:

Even though Pauline was only 19, her maturity was much older than that, even on the sexual side of our relationship. She even persuaded me to make love to her in the middle of a park in the middle of a sunny Sunday afternoon, and even in the toilets of a crowded pub. Things I would never think of doing!

I also gained the experience of being completely in love, which I wouldn't have missed. He was very passionate about me and this gave me a tremendous sense of physical and sexual confidence, which has lasted. He was far less sexually experienced than I am, despite the age difference, and it gave me a great deal of assurance to be so successful in the role of teacher.
(woman younger by 16 years)

I don't know whether I'm proud or ashamed to tell you that I was the first woman he'd had. He was completely inexperienced so I had to teach him absolutely everything. But it has been magical. I don't know really whether I say that because it gives me a feeling of control. I suppose I'm afraid that he may want to go off to try it with someone else, but he says no because our sex life is so fantastic it could never be better or as good with anyone else. And of course he is without doubt the best I've ever had, because the joy of discovery for him is backed up by the virility and stamina of a 21-year-old.

For others, though, having such an inexperienced partner did not always turn out quite so happily:

He was only 16 when we got together and of course was completely inexperienced. At first it was very exciting because I was still married, so we had to take opportunities where we could and you know how that lends flavour to anything. By the time we were married it had calmed down to a normal sort of sex life, but it gradually tailed off over the years until we had no sex at all. I can't believe I was so naïve but in fact it has turned out that he is gay. He just didn't have time to understand himself before we were embarked on this mad sexual fling but, as he puts it now rather cruelly, that was just like a teenager masturbating. It wasn't what he really felt sexually; he only found that out later and it wasn't women that he wanted, it was fellas. He was actually meeting blokes in clubs and even in loos for several years before I found out.

For many people who had previously been married for some years, they felt that their sexual growth had stopped or moved on only very slowly during this time, so that the expectations and activities of the new, younger partner were a revelation to them!

Vicky, on her previous older partners:

I realize now there's something about that generation of men brought up in the 1930s and 1940s, and oral sex. It was suppressed at that time – oral sex was 'yuck' as far as women were concerned. If they could find younger women who were exploring their sexuality and would do it or allow it, then that was a major thing: 'This is so fantastic, are you sure?', etc. Their wives were on a pedestal and our sex lives became geared around oral or adventurous sex because they could get, or had had, ordinary sex at home with the wife.

The thing that made me realize that I wasn't past it sexually was that I was able to make love to Dawn twice in a row with hardly a pause. I hadn't ever done that in my marriage, not even when we were much younger, and I realize now that was a sort of learned pattern from my wife. Without ever saying so, she made it absolutely clear that once was enough and there was neither expectation of, nor desire for, a second attempt. Consequently I thought I'd be incapable of it until Dawn made it clear that her expectations and desires were quite, quite different.

Different Levels of Desire

It is often assumed that sexual desire decreases with age as does performance level. This may be the result of the widely known fact that men reach their sexual peak at about 17 and women not until they are around 40 . . . a good argument for older-woman age gap relationships if ever we heard one!

Sex is a problem in that he does not have the same level of sexual desire as I do, but it is difficult to know if this is really a manifestation of age or if he has always had a low sex drive. This has meant that I have indulged in several extra-relationship affairs which were purely for sex. I would never tell him because he would be very upset and feel that it was his fault that he had let me down by not keeping me satisfied. I know that line sounds like the

perfect cop-out for a woman having a series of meaning-
less affairs, but I do honestly believe it to be true.

But it would be wrong to assume that it is the younger partner
who always has a stronger sex drive than the older, as this
example shows:

When I first met Phillip I was very flattered by how often he
wanted to have sex with me. I wasn't that experienced but
the other men I'd been with had nothing like his level of
activity. He wanted sex literally every night, which I found
surprising in a man of 45. I gave birth to twins not long after
we were married and was completely exhausted by it, but
there was no question of him taking this into account. On
the day I came back from my postnatal examination, he
was determined to start our active sex life again and from
that day until he had a serious illness 15 years later there
was literally no let-up. It was sex at least once a day, except I
had five days off for my period. Then he even said that he
saw no reason why my period should stop us. But I drew
the line at that. I know many people would be surprised
about his level of desire because you'd expect his powers to
wane as he gets older, but they don't. But the way he keeps
his interest is not right, to my mind. Although he wants sex
so much, he is not open and relaxed about it. Sex is dirty to
him and the dirtiness is what turns him on. He likes to
watch other people, for example, and fantasizes about
them. I'm ashamed to say this but he even bought binocu-
lars so that he could watch our neighbours' teenage
daughters – they both have big breasts – sunbathing and
then he gets all excited and wants sex with me. I am sure
this attitude is to do with his age, as he was brought up in a
time when sex was considered dirty and he learned to be
excited by things like that. A year ago I started an affair with
a man of my age and it has been a revelation that, to him,
sex is funny and easy, not forbidden.

After the first baby there was less and less sexual activity: I was too tired and he was not interested. By accident our second child was conceived, but after he was born, sexual activity never really resumed, and I was bitter and angry. He would not talk to the doctor or go to marriage guidance, implying that it was my fault that I had become unattractive and he could do nothing to help. I became miserable . . .

However, where the communication in the relationship remained good, the partners did not feel that the different levels of desire was an insurmountable problem at all, although they did acknowledge its existence.

Different Sexual Manners

Here's Maurice on a relationship he had with a woman 20 years younger than himself:

Sex was a problem, I will admit. It wasn't so much that we were incompatible . . . at least not in the physical sense. It was more about the manners of sex, if you follow me. We sort of had different ideas about what it should be like and what the expectations were. I like long sex . . . You know, over a long period of time during which you might stop for a bit, have a glass of wine, a smoke, a chat. But of course with her age-group you have to use a condom nowadays and this is really a problem for me because the way I like to have sex my erection comes and goes. Of course that is a problem with a condom, because it slips off and you can't get it back on so you have to use another and somehow there is the expectation that once you put this thing on you mean business — you know, you are going for it — whereas I like orgasms to take me by surprise.

Practically the same phrase was used by Alistair:

> You could never say her orgasms took her by surprise; it was a very serious affair, having to make sure she was OK. I don't mean to be sexist but I found this quite a problem, this ensuring equal – no, more than equal – satisfaction for her. She was very unforgiving if I didn't. I'm sure that is only fair and right but it isn't easy for an old stager like me. God. I had a relationship for five years with a woman who had never had an orgasm in her life and she didn't seem to mind. She always said she enjoyed it. Mind you, she never initiated it. These young women, though, they wouldn't put up with that . . . they want what they want and how they want it and they've got us men to feel that if they don't come it's our fault because we are not good enough.

> His Austrian Catholic background . . . along with what seemed to me some attitudes from another time, meant that he found me and my very different assumptions exciting and also shocking. I liked this situation very much, basically, I think, because it made us more equal in power.

Women did not seem to be shy about making the first move. According to one older woman:

> Our sexual relationship, which it was very obvious we both wanted, actually began at my instigation, when I invited him to my flat for dinner and really went for it. That nerve-racking experience gave me a lot of sympathy for men, who are generally still expected to make the running in this area.

Younger ones, too, were not afraid to go for it:

One night he asked me out for a drink insisting that his intentions were honourable, and I made the first move.

Some people expressed concern about the ageing process and the effect it might have on their sex lives:

Ian also had doubts about his attractiveness to me because of his age, and I found this touching.

One disadvantage we anticipated is that our sex life would diminish because of my failing powers. This has not yet happened. If and when it does, perhaps our needs won't be so great anyway.

This last admission was said in almost identical words by at least two others, and similar sentiments were expressed by half a dozen other interviewees.

Certainly most of our respondents would echo Howard's words:

What I've learned above all since Jan and I have been together is that sex is not about smooth and perfect bodies and prescribed ways of doing it. If you think like that it will always become boring eventually. It is about sharing feelings and being confident in the relationship, never feeling you have to prove anything, about total acceptance and trust. Put like that, it sounds not very exciting, but I can only say it is, very!

When so much of people's sex lives seems to be fraught with difficulty, it was very heartwarming to hear the sheer joy with which people like Helen described their experiences:

I was walking with a girl friend through an old village on one of the Greek islands and we had knocked on a door to ask for water ... The lady called upstairs several times and eventually down came this beautiful creature — Demetrios — like an incarnation of the god Pan — with liquid brown eyes. I was pierced . . . We met accidentally twice more on successive nights at a bar and I thought, 'He can't be interested in me, I'm old enough to be his mother.' But then he took me back to his house. Up into his attic bedroom, where he had a wonderful iron bed — a four-poster, all hung with curtains — very old. He said, 'You want make love with me' after he had kissed me — kisses that went through me like a knife. I got into bed with him and had the experience of being adored, like the words of the marriage service 'with my body I thee worship'. He was only 24 years old but he had control of his body. He could go a long time. I stayed the night but was worried that his parents would be upset. However, they just seemed to accept it and a few days later I moved in with him. Into the room with the four-poster bed and wooden floorboards and windows in two of the walls that both looked out on the sea. A room with white crushed walls, all uneven. Into this Greek world the whole thing had the quality of myth — of dream and magic. We were in bed all the time — only leaving it to go to the beach and to go out at night with his friends. I was 47, but nobody seemed to realize or think anything of it. Most days we must have made love about ten times. He was never tired. He didn't want me to wash, but when we did it was in a big plastic tub — there was no shower — no bath with taps. I washed him and he washed me but he liked the smell of my body and didn't want it washed off that often. After three weeks there, I had to return to Athens. But I returned within a week.

6

Short-term Relationships

So far we have concentrated upon what one might refer to as 'proper couples'. Many age gap relationships are of short duration but are nonetheless significant for the participants – either at the time they occur or sometimes for longer – because of the effect the relationship had on their lives.

Some of these relationships were truly short-term in that they lasted only a few weeks or months. Some went on longer, a year or more, sometimes several years. The common thing about many of them is that neither partner had any expectation that they would develop into permanent relationships. Of course several interviewees, who had started out feeling that their age gap relationship would be like that, found that it developed otherwise! The experiences reviewed here are from those relationships which did not develop but which left their mark all the same.

Here's one response from a woman who had a relationship with a man 20 years her junior:

Everyone should have one at least once in their lives, that's my firm belief.

and:

Ultimately it was right that we split up, but I wouldn't have missed the experience of that fresh young thing for all the tea in China.

This was said with feeling by a man recalling a relationship he had many years previously with a woman 30 years younger. While several of our interviewees' short-term relationships had taken place years, or even decades, in the past, we were left with the distinct impression that such affairs are probably more common now:

> Since nowadays marriages can easily be ended, one does not feel bound by one's marriage vows. The knowledge that you can end a relationship is a valuable and comforting fact. It must have been awful in the olden days when divorce was unusual and one knew that only death would set one free.

> We both knew it was strictly a short-term thing and that gave it added poignancy and pleasure.

Easier divorce and a more relaxed attitude to cohabitation mean that people can sample a relationship they would not try if it meant permanent commitment. The ease of gaining a divorce also means more people have been through a marriage and children, and are now ready for what they may see as a less committed relationship, or one where the potential for producing a family is of lesser consequence than the pure enjoyment of the other person's company. Conventions and expectations of suitable partners can much more easily be swept aside. The short-term nature also means the partners can take from it what is right for them without worrying about longer-term compatibility. Some will risk a large age gap with an affair that they wouldn't risk if they thought it was going to be a long-term relationship.

> The age gap didn't matter in our affair because it was an affair. My family and friends didn't know about it because he was married, and that was always much more important than the age difference.

What people said they gained from these short-term relationships was that:

- They had fun.
- They had new and unexpected experiences.
- They gained knowledge which was important to them at other stages of their lives.

Fun and Freedom

The knowledge that it could never be permanent was so freeing. The whole thing was just so light-hearted. Everything had some kind of special focus because you knew it might not be repeated.

Some people find the expectations and pressures within peer partnerships confining. Stepping outside your own age-group can release you from those expectations and either open doors for new experiences or behaviour, or free you to make choices and decisions that feel right for you without the guilt that you ought to be marrying or making a commitment, or simply do not enjoy multiple partners. Age gap relationships offer a freedom of behaviour for some people.

The relationship just corresponded to my emotional needs at the time; in other words, a need for a father-figure coupled with the desire to live on my own with only a part-time relationship.
(younger woman)

Because I'd been brought up in this very religious household where marriage was everything, I found going out with girls of my own age very stressful because I felt they were always sizing me up as a marriage partner. And I was doing the same of course, and usually running a mile from the prospect and then feeling very full of guilt because I had, from the family's perception, 'abandoned' them. When I met Flora it was like a great release because she obviously didn't want to marry anybody, she'd been married for 20 years and had three kids. So we were just able to enjoy being together without any expectations. It made everything so easy. That applied to sex especially, though it took me a while to learn that it was fine just to enjoy fucking without having to feel you must marry the person.

For some people the slightly clandestine nature of the relation-ship, which was brought about because of the difference in age, added greatly to the fun.

Pretending that we hardly knew each other when we met socially was a great laugh. We would catch each other's eye across a room and share a secret glance and then laugh like hell about it when we were alone.

I met him when he came to give me an estimate for deco-rating my dining-room and it went on from there. We used to go to bed in the afternoon while the kids were at school in a very secretive way. I used to stand at the school gates afterwards wondering how many of the other mums had just left the bed of their much younger lover.

For many, the experience of an age gap lover was very much a healing or restoring confidence experience.

My husband left me to go off with someone else when I was nearly 40. I'd literally not had another lover apart from him, not even a serious boyfriend really. All my sexual experience had been with him and when he left I suppose I imagined that I'd never have another man at all.

I just devoted all my energy to looking after the children and trying to cope with my own feelings of hurt and rejection. After a couple of years I started going to this evening class and came across this sweet young man called Geoffrey. He seemed very interested in me, always wanting to sit near me and so on. After a few weeks he asked me to have a drink with him after the class and this became a regular event. Then he started coming round to my house occasionally and ringing me up for a chat. I realize now that he was 'courting' me or chatting me up, but at the time I simply didn't put that connotation on it. Because he was 15 years younger, it never occurred to me he was interested in me that way and I was of course completely out of the habit of thinking of myself as in any way sexually attractive. I am not sure how long this would have gone on because I'm sure he'd have got fed up with my lack of response, but a friend said that she thought he fancied me and that I should at least give him an opportunity. I got a bit drunk the next time he came round and asked him straight out if he wanted to go to bed ... I can't think how I had the nerve. His reply was something like 'I thought you'd never ask!' We were in bed in less time than it takes to tell. I just couldn't believe what fun the sex was and I particularly couldn't get over how he fancied me. No sooner had we finished one session than he was ready to start again! The relationship went on for about a year altogether. Neither of us expected it to be permanent but I'll always be grateful for him giving me back my confidence in myself as a woman.

Some people deliberately seek a short-term relationship at a particular point in their lives, but it was rare for our respondents actively to seek a relationship with a much older or younger lover. Rather they happened by accident and gave them experiences they would never dream of having:

Unexpected Experiences

I liked older men then as I needed a father-figure as well as a lover; I wasn't ready for marriage and settling down until much later. I also felt drawn to their greater experience and knowledge.

Several interviewees felt grateful for having been able to experience things which hitherto had been outside their range. This may have been because they had not met anyone previously who had been, for example, an *aficionado* of the opera or greyhound racing.

All my friends were going to discos but I was going to opera, and it gave me such a buzz. Julia introduced me to things it would have taken me years to discover on my own.

He gave me a glimpse of another world really. He bought me sports cars. We used to spend a lot of time in gentlemen's clubs, drinking with actors and various luvvies. We had fantastic holidays in the kind of lifestyle of Grand Lux hotels in Europe.

It was also among this group of people that we found the issue of class seemed most strongly significant.

Twenty years ago I was in PR and in regular contact with a catering manager who was 12 years younger. He fell in love with me and I went along with it partly because I was flattered – he was very handsome – and partly for sex. But he grew jealous, made scenes, embarrassed me. My friends were snooty – he was not an educated man and did not fit in, and my children didn't like him either – they were old enough to know that he was different and had a

Cockney accent. I know that I treated him badly and in effect used him – he was a willing slave.

I remember the shock I felt when I first heard him refer to me as his 'girlfriend'. He was on the phone to someone and I heard him use the expression. I looked at him, this beautiful young car mechanic in my hallway. A car mechanic when I'd only had academics before and thought, 'His girlfriend?' Well, I suppose I am!

The acknowledged short-term nature of the relationship freed people to make more cross-class relationships than is usual in our class-ridden society. This did not only apply to the UK, since several of the people we interviewed were from the US.

The phenomenon of 'a bit of rough' or 'down-dating' has had currency in the US for some while and seems to be spreading rapidly. As women feel more free to say that they want a man for his body not his mind, they also grow more confident about making a pass at, say, the plumber.

He was mending my sink when I suddenly noticed what a nice bum he had. I knew he wouldn't approach me because he'd find me too frightening so I made all the running. I thought, 'Thank God for a man I won't have to talk to after we have had sex.' We had rather a laugh when he went to a fancy dress party with me on New Year's Eve as 'a bit of rough'. My posh girlfriends couldn't keep their hands off him.

Learning for the Rest of One's Life

Though some of our interviewees' relationships were quite a long time earlier, many had had a lasting effect, providing them with a learning experience, or a template for relationships or skills, which were of value to them for the rest of their lives.

> He met my emotional need at the time but also taught me such a lot about emotions and feelings. I am quite a different person because of him, richer emotionally, deeper and more fulfilled.

> I don't exaggerate when I say she changed my life. My expectations of others are different and my ability to give adequately within my family setting is immeasurably increased because of my year with her.

Some of our interviewees felt that they learned an entirely new way of relating to people because of their age gap relationship.

> I was talking to my flatmate one night and I realized that it was the first time I had ever talked to him and actually heard him, understood him I mean. Before that, we had exchanged information necessary to live together but I had never really cared about his views on anything. I realize that I had learned this interest in people and real concern for them from June, because that is how she related to people. That is a skill I hope I'll keep all my life.

The fact that they valued the skills learned did not stop the participants feeling pain and anxiety when the relationship came to an end, and the age gap sometimes made the ending all the more poignant.

The End of the Relationship

When we split up, he would tell you I threw him out; I say he left me, so perhaps it was a bit of both. We had a huge argument because he invited some people I didn't know to stay in my one-bedroom flat without asking me first. The next day he was returning to Moscow for a month, and although I thought he might not come back, only when he wrote telling me to pack and keep his belongings did I realize that the break was permanent. I had not wanted to end the relationship in such an unamicable way and felt both abandoned and insulted by his entreaties to care for his belongings. I was traumatized by the loss of this relationship and it took two years to get over it. Now, of course, I realize that I had in fact been fed up with him but too frightened of loneliness to get rid of him – or even admit this to myself. Certainly the relationship carried on far too long, but it's not so easy to split up if you're cohabiting.

When we split up I was absolutely devastated, totally wrecked and cried all the time for about two years.

When the relationship ended I felt I had lost everything. I was utterly devastated and suffered from months of depression. Eighteen months later I have at last begun to feel I am getting over it and have begun a relationship with someone else. I do not yet feel ready for anything serious.

Splitting up is often the time when you have to face the comments about being with an older/younger partner from friends who have up till now kept quiet. They may point out that you have wasted your time, almost saying 'I told you so.'

I wouldn't now not have done it, but my mother when we split up said 'What a terrible waste of three years,' and I was furious with her for saying that, for even though I was in the slough of despond I realized that, no, there were good things to it.

I should have listened to my friends more because they were proved right in the end.

In spite of the pain caused at the end several interviewees said they felt it helped them move on to another relationship, even though it made them wary:

I was always a very idealistic person who wanted to have intense romantic relationships and believed it would all end when I found true love. I don't think that at all now. I suppose I still think I'll end up with someone who's (hopefully) permanent, but it's not the assumption that it used to be, and I don't make the assumptions I used to about what the relationship will be like. I don't know if this is a loss or a gain, but no one will take me for a ride again and get away with it.
(older woman)

There is no comparison with other relationships – it was both indescribably better and indescribably worse. I have never been so in love with anybody and it was by far the most intense and passionate relationship I have ever had. I have also never been so hurt by anyone and I would be wary of ever getting involved with someone at that deep level again because the risk is so great.
(younger woman)

Staying Friends

Inevitably, as we have seen above, some of the relationships ended in tears. Usually this was because the people concerned did not agree about the right time to end, though in these short-term relationships there was usually an understanding that an end would come eventually.

However, most of the endings were well-managed and — where we were told of an age gap relationship several or many years previously — many of the former couples had stayed friends. They saw each other through new relationships, became family friends at later times, even godparents to children when they came along in their ex-partner's new relationship.

Clearly, in many cases what the partners had gained from the pairing was sufficiently important for both of them to last beyond the sexual element of the relationship, and friendships remained after the ending of the sexual partnership:

> I have never felt anything but warm towards him, and like his now-wife enormously. They come to stay with me and, all credit to her, she always seems entirely accepting of me.
> (older woman)

> She actually lives in the same village as me now. We always kept in touch, we went to her wedding and when she and James were house-hunting it seemed natural to tell them about the house for sale very near to us.
> (older man)

> I introduced him to the woman he eventually married, as I was convinced they were right for each other. When she finally became pregnant after a very difficult time of treatment for infertility, I was the first person they rang to give the news.
> (older woman)

Some people may say that the woman above was merely continuing to do what she had always done for the young man: act as his mother. But from what was reported to us, there often seemed to be great affection and warmth remaining once the relationship had ended and those feelings also extended to the new partner. It may be that the (older) ex-partner is not seen as a rival, which is sometimes the case in 'normal', non-age gap relationships when these finish.

The Down Side

However, it would be wrong to give the impression that all was entirely sweetness and light when our interviewees' short-term relationships ended. Some felt the relationship had had an unwelcome knock-on effect on their lives.

The trouble is, I can never find a woman of my own age to compare with her. I badly want to marry and have children but every likely candidate I meet I measure them against Elaine. Of course I'm asking the impossible because a woman of my age could not possibly have had all her experience.

That man met all my needs and I feel no one can ever do that again. All the men I meet that I'd like to marry, or who would like to marry me, seem gauche and immature beside him.

When I was 19 I fell in love with a married man of 40 and our affair lasted for five years. After a few months I grew depressed, as I felt we had no real future, and tried to kill myself. At 25 I fell for another man who was 55 and began a relationship which lasted six years . . . I liked their experience and understanding and learned a great deal from both these men. They deepened my cultural life, had a fund of life experience and appreciated my youth. The second relationship ended gradually when I again reached the stage of feeling there was no future in it, and I was getting older and perhaps feeling I may want to have children, which would not have been possible with a partner so much older.

I was 34 when it started and Gerard was 53 . . . The relationship lasted for about nine years. It never really came to any kind of recognizable end. It just sort of petered out over the last few years. I think that my fear of being confronted with Gerard's ageing and death was subconsciously at work, putting a serious damper on things.

Sometimes this led the participants to question themselves and their judgements:

It's all very well me saying I split up with him because I wanted to marry and have kids, but I have set up a situation for myself where that seems impossible because of the relationship I had with him and nothing else being half so good. Is that an accident, a coincidence, or have I set it up?

So the best outcome of a short-term, age gap relationship seems to be that they felt better equipped for the rest of their lives, and the worst that they felt less well-equipped as a result of it. However, from our sample, the former experience was far more frequent than the latter. Even where they were painful, the experiences reported to us were seen as valuable, and most interviewees felt like Frank:

I wouldn't have missed it for the world.

or like Christine:

I had never thought about age gap relationships before and never considered having one, but there was something about it which felt so reassuring to me. I would certainly (carefully) enter another; in fact this is a very appealing idea and I would very much like to. It felt like home.

7

Gains and Losses

Such is the apparent premium placed on youth in our society that it has always been suggested — both in the media and to us — that all the gains in age gap relationships are for the older partner, with the implication that they had somehow, by their cunning and deviousness, hoodwinked the younger partner. This was certainly not the impression we gained! We asked all our interviewees if they could sum up the advantages and disadvantages of an age gap relationship from their own point of view. So many more plus points were cited by the younger partners that we will start with what they had to say.

The Younger Partner

Knowledge and Experience

First was the advantage of being with someone whose knowledge and experience was wider than theirs.

It is a definite advantage to be around somebody who has, because of their age, such a different experience of life. I find that I can learn many things from him.

For me a relationship must be based largely on companionship and intelligent conversation, and so far I've found older men have more to offer. On the whole, I find them more well-rounded people, less macho and competitive, more thoughtful, caring lovers — they are more concerned with you as a person than with trying to get their end away.

He introduced me to brown rice, feminism and the arts, and told me the music I liked so much but couldn't name was from *The Threepenny Opera* by Brecht and Weill. The relationship provided a useful short-cut to highbrow stuff to me who was interested but without a source of information until then. I became a sort of protégée and I still think that without his help and encouragement I would not have pursued my studies so effectively — although I was getting good marks, I still thought I was stupid. He also encouraged me to travel which I wanted to do but was too timid, and he gave me the confidence to embark on journeys around Turkey, Israel and America on my own. Again it was because of his confidence in my abilities that I continued on to a postgrad degree — it would never have occurred to me that I was clever enough.

It is not the case that younger partners were simply naïve and awestruck with their partners. What they expressed was an appreciation of being able to profit from the experience of their older partner. This gave an added value to the relationship and they were able to develop extra skills and knowledge in themselves.

I liked the idea of a 'mentor', I suppose, and enjoyed listening to these men's experience in their lives — people they had met, things they had done, travels and adventures they had lived through.

I found him fascinating because of the wealth of experience he had that was far outside my own. He had travelled extensively; his house was full of interesting objects; he was interested in art and music and had friends in these fields. I found it both exciting and peaceful to be with him.

A gay man said:

He gave me access to a very wide range of new experiences, with a guiding hand when needed.

The age gap was the short-cut to these new experiences, and it was this fact that was appreciated.

Emotional Security

Being loved by someone older also brought the advantage of greater emotional security.

He had had a strong marriage for 39 years and was ready to transfer his affections to me. He was a 'man of the world' and intelligent. He had a stable income, occupational pension and his own house.

The older partner was often felt more able to be supportive in times of stress. Tim, for example, says that:

When my mother was in her last illness, and after she died, I felt that Posy pulled me through: without her stability, I would have been lost and so alone.

There was also a valued freedom and sense of independence resulting from the greater emotional security afforded by having an older partner:

We each married for friendship and companionship and that has been totally fulfilled.

He gave me a stability I had never had before, and I could always call on his advice and help without ever feeling inadequate or stupid. He always encouraged me in whatever I felt I wanted to do. An age gap mellows a partner a great deal.

Generally the emotional pay-off was in what they themselves gained as a result:

The fact that he loved me helped me to gain a self-confidence that I had not had before. Pete's legacy to me is largely an intangible one – mainly in terms of self-confidence – and it is a very valuable legacy.

Feeling Special

Everyone in love has that feeling of being particularly special. We sensed that, for the younger partners, getting attention from an older partner gave the relationship an extra dimension:

Feeling thrilled and excited at the specialness of us being together.

... that someone who is looked up to and revered because of age and status might be interested in me.

I found him charming, witty and charismatic, but I didn't think for a moment that he would be interested in someone who was (then) exactly half his age.

This overall feeling was summed up by one person, who said:

She gave me a feeling of self-worth; gave me self-esteem and inspiration.

Sex

Although we have already looked at this in Chapter 5, the sexual gains to be had from having an older partner were frequently mentioned by the younger partners we interviewed:

> She did teach me to be a considerate lover and made up for my lack of sex education and training!

> Pete took me away for dirty weekends – it was fun, doing something so wanton and extravagant. We've been to many hotels in the north of England from Scunthorpe to Alnmouth, and no doubt left a string of raised eyebrows along the way. Even now, you can see people scrutinizing us in the pubs trying to work out exactly what relationship we are to one another . . . The first few months of our meeting were the most exciting time I've ever had . . . We still go to hotels now and Pete recently bought me a car so we can travel further afield and shock more satisfied communities. How many young girls in my situation can boast that?

Material Benefits

Younger partners mentioned the material benefits of an older partner as well.

> We had marvellous holidays and in general enjoyed a much better standard of living than I had been used to . . . I have to admit that if he had been, say, uneducated and unemployed and living in a deprived area I don't think I would have been so interested in him.

> I found greater security for myself than I'd experienced before. I certainly enjoyed having a home of my own and being able to entertain when and whom I wished.

The advantages of the 'sugar daddy' are enormous (no puns intended). There's an old cliché that goes 'Better to be an old man's darling than a young man's slave' which like all clichés has some truth in it. For the most part I am treated like a queen, given all the attention and material comforts I could wish for. And, although I'm no material girl, I have to admit that, as a poor student, I became the envy of my flatmates when I was whisked off to four star hotels and posh restaurants, given clothes and chocolates and flowers galore.

This was also expressed by one of the gay men we spoke to:

Latterly the lush lifestyle he could give me was a great bonus.

Younger partners were no more or less gold-diggers than anyone else but they were aware that financial security, if not a prerequisite for happiness, can certainly help things along!

Although the comments above are only a summary, overall our younger partners unquestionably felt they were getting a very good deal from their age gap partners. They had gained in knowledge, confidence, security, experience and more, with the sense – although it can never be compared – that this was more than might have been from a same age partnership. But the experiences of relationships, alas, don't come in two distinct columns headed 'plus' and 'minus':

Since I also learned a lot from him which would have taken longer on my own, it's impossible for me to weigh up the advantages and disadvantages – there were a lot of both.

Younger partners, inevitably, felt there were also disadvantages linked to having a much older partner. Some of these are listed below.

Different Outlooks

The same difference in experience and attitude that could be so stimulating could also be a source of frustration:

> It is still hard sometimes when I want to do things I class as fun, like ice-skating or camping and he thinks it is just childish.

> He wants different things out of life: a home, children and all the trappings that go with it and I hated the idea of having a baby and giving up my career. Now I am a bit older myself I want the same things as Derek . . . When we used to fight he would always call me immature or tell me to grow up – what he didn't seem to realize was that I was only a teenager and I knew I still had a lot of growing up to do. We can't be 40 overnight, can we?

They also reported regret when the older partner did not seem to take the younger one seriously just because of the age factor:

> I wonder now whether he perceived me as too young to take seriously (I find this very painful if true). Maybe he believed that someone my age couldn't be looking for a lasting commitment, so he couldn't really hurt or disappoint me, but I was 27 not 21.

As time passes, an age gap which initially seemed unimportant may start to present problems:

> I never saw the problem looming up but now that Phillip has retired he wants me to be at home with him, whereas I'm just getting a second wind in my career. The 17 years between us has never seemed more of a gulf.

Lack of Shared Experience

As we said in Chapter 2, lack of shared experience prompted some concern and proved to be a possible source of conflict within the relationship:

> If I had to list the disadvantages of having a 'sugar daddy', I think the main one would be jealousy of his past. The fact that he had a whole life of his own before I was even born is quite an alarming thought. Occasionally, I think I'm too inexperienced compared with him and his count- less girlfriends (he was at Sussex University in the promis- cuous 1970s). That mysterious 20 year gap sometimes haunts me — I feel there is just a little part of him that I can never know, and it saddens me.

> It can be very difficult if you spend time thinking about the fact that your partner was out at work when you were born and his best friends have children not much younger than yourself . . . It can be rather depressing to think of all the things you haven't shared in his life, all the places he has been without you, all the people he has met and all the ideas and dreams he has lived out.

Not having shared the experience was one problem. Another was the feeling of inadequacy which the greater experience of the older partner could generate in the younger one:

> Sometimes I worry that I'm not as smart as he is, and don't stimulate him enough intellectually. I know what he has to offer me — experience, knowledge, informed conversa- tion, but what can I give in return?

> If I've lost anything from dating an older woman, it must be a little innocence. I feel wiser and less naïve, just from the two years I've known her. Sometimes I wonder what

I'd have been getting up to in my final year at university if I hadn't been so smitten with my new girlfriend, but I have no regrets.

My other relationships have been with men my own age and who therefore have similar levels of responsibility at work to mine. Luke was far more senior and I found it very difficult to insist that he put arrangements with me before levels of responsibility much higher than my own. For example, he was always late when we met (which I believe is a form of passive aggression), but I couldn't assert myself because of what he'd been doing and had to accept it when he said he couldn't finish earlier . . . I have never put up with it from anyone else. I suppose being in love itself can make you act untypically – I'm quite a decisive and articulate person, but I wasn't with him.

Without careful and considerate handling, it seems that the younger partner could be left feeling inadequate and lacking in confidence.

Families and Friends

Younger partners often sacrificed their own friends because it was difficult to integrate the two sets (see also Chapter 3).

I had to lose touch with friends as he was quite possessive and people of his generation have more expectation that their woman should devote the whole of their lives to their man.

I lost contact with my contemporaries and the relationship took me out of my sphere. I found I was cutting myself off from them.

A generation gap could feel a drawback when it came to families. This could be because the two partners have different expectations about child care:

> With our second child I didn't get a lot of practical help from Vic because men of his generation did not expect to do much in the way of baby care.

It might also be because there are problems with teenagers:

> When our younger son was a teenager the age gap really caused problems because Victor was then in his seventies and couldn't really cope with a teenage son, so, needless to say, I had to cope with a few more problems. Was he safe borrowing the car? Was he out underage drinking? Victor tended not to see that there were any problems at all. This made me feel resentful and alienated. I felt we were leading separate lives and wanted to talk about it, but he would not acknowledge that there were any problems.

These problems could result because the younger partner may miss out on the experience of being a parent, and some, inevitably, have feelings of regret:

> I thought it would never matter that I could never have my own children because Moira was so much older, but now that I am pretty well too old myself, I do wonder.

> I feel he has lost the chance to have the excitement of kids in his life. He loves kids and would have liked them.

Separation

The disadvantage mentioned most frequently by younger partners did not concern the present, but the future. Their concerns revolved around the effects of ageing and the fear of separation through death. These fears are understandably more acute in partners who are considerably younger.

> His heart attack made me realize he was getting on and vulnerable. The long-term result has been that he can no longer do strenuous things like long walks in the country or some forms of gardening, so I do them on my own or with friends. The increasing years have made him less tolerant, less able to make allowances, for example, with things we watch on TV, listen on the radio or read.

This physical deterioration, especially if accompanied by mental atrophy, was also a source of fear:

> I may become a young widow, or worse a full-time nurse as he deteriorates.

> I had to hold back on some of my more energetic habits because he couldn't keep up either physically or mentally.

Although the younger partners did not expressly mention this to us, the older partners sometimes articulated on their partners' behalf anxieties about the physical effects of ageing on the body, and how these changes might affect them:

> I am feeling very bad about my body which is deteriorating quickly, but he swears he sees none of it . . . He says it doesn't matter, but he may resent it some time, especially as I grow uglier.

There were poignant expressions of the fear of loss felt by the younger partners:

> My one regret is that, inevitably perhaps, our time together doesn't stretch before us. Selfishly, I want to do

everything with Dave now; I don't and can't wait until we've had children and they've left home. Whenever I catch myself dwelling on this fact I remind myself that life doesn't come with a guarantee; there could be a bus coming round the corner to strike you down, whatever your age.

A disadvantage of the relationship is that I worry that I am going to be left on my own when he dies, as logically he will die 10 to 20 years before me. I wish I had met him earlier in our lives ...

What I hadn't expected was a great sense of loss that I would probably never have 40 years of marriage with him, that he will probably die before me.

Despite these worries we gained a clear sense of overall gain from our younger partner interviewees. Few seemed to doubt they had made the right decision and come out a winner:

I would never change it, looking back. It has been a lot more pluses than minuses.

These advantages for the younger partner outweighed the disadvantages numerically, despite conventional wisdom. These plus points also appeared to outnumber the advantages for the older partner.

The Older Partner

Of course there are problems making generalized statements about the advantages gained for any partner, because one person's advantage can be another's disadvantage:

I was getting the best of the bargain, a vigorous young man at the beginning of his career with a great future before him.

or:

I exchanged a well-established husband with secure prospects for the uncertainty of one who was starting out, and that wasn't easy.

In contrast to those for younger partners, only two principal advantages were cited by older partners.

Staying Younger Longer

I've gained by our relationship because she brought youth and enthusiasm to me; she loves to have fun and be silly and I'd almost forgotten how to laugh.

The advantages I think are mostly mine, although he very kindly thinks he has many. My own feelings about this relationship are only joy and gratitude because he has stopped me becoming a dried-up, lonely crone and I feel 20 years younger.

Most people want to retain their youth, if not actually then at least psychologically. You may not want to be Dorian Gray but neither do you want to become Methuselah. One way of doing this seems to be to acquire a younger partner. You may then acquire younger friends, a more youthful outlook, take on new interests and so on. Of course you have to contribute to this: you have to be prepared to go along with the younger outlook and to be open to new interests. Brenda was described by her younger partner thus:

She is the sort of person who, when you tell her a change is going to happen – to the home, in the workplace or anything – doesn't react like most people with a knee-jerk reaction against the very idea, but rather will greet it with an expression like 'Isn't that exciting?'

If this is the way you are, as the older partner, then the rewards can be considerable.

He had access to my younger world and friends and that kept him young.
(gay man)

It need not be just about friends and stimulation but about the joy of seeing a younger person grow and develop, as the man above continued:

He had a front row seat at the panto of seven or eight years of my growing and changing so rapidly.

Kudos, Trophies and Toy Boys

The older partners we spoke with were frank about the kudos they felt they gained from a younger partner:

There was undoubtedly a social cachet to be derived from 'having a younger woman'. It also kept me on my mettle, even to developing interests in other kinds of music, theatre and the arts than those I'd had before. I enjoyed having a ready-made daughter of my own, too, and was very rarely conscious of the fact that I wasn't her father.

I noticed the people at the office look at me with new respect and interest after he'd called to collect me. I think they thought I was past it and they were impressed that, not only was I not past it, but could get someone as young and dishy as him.

or, as their partners saw it:

He was acquiring a younger healthy wife with her own house and income but also someone good-looking to have on his arm.

The phenomenon of a trophy wife is well known and, although not cited as a main reason by the older men we interviewed, it was certainly seen as a desirable bonus.

It gave me back some sense of pride in myself which I'd largely lost when my marriage broke up.

One older man said his wife was always telling him how lucky he was:

No children; no pets; all the bills halved; a wife who won't spend money on the house – she always tells me that I'm in heaven, that I have all the advantages of marriage without any of the expense and inconveniences!

Like this man, many of our older partners felt they had made a very good deal indeed and saw the personal pride they gained from the sense of having 'caught' a younger partner as an added bonus.

The same applied for the older women we spoke to. However, they could feel that the force of social convention and pride in having a younger man was mixed with some embarrassment about what people might think:

I did worry they were laughing behind their hands at me.

Only two basic disadvantages were reported by older partners.

Feeling Inadequate

Some of the older partners said they feared feeling inadequate. This might concern their opinions:

> As an older person I feel I may have opinions which are not politically correct — out of step with the views of her generation.

A few feared being left by the younger partner for a person more their own age:

> A disadvantage is my insecurity when a younger woman talks to my husband. After eight years of marriage, I am only just beginning to cope with this.

or, as in a couple of unsuccessful partnerships:

> Basically I put up with his awful behaviour, his actual and verbal violence when he insulted me as well as beat me, because I was simply petrified of him going off with a younger woman. Somehow it would be worse to be left in those circumstances than when my husband left me. He went off with another woman but, because she was the same age as me, it didn't feel quite so humiliating. No one was going to whisper behind their hands about me being a foolish old woman taken for a ride by this brash young man.

The second disadvantage related to the down side of staying younger longer (which was seen as an advantage). This was the fear of always having to keep up with their partner.

Trying to Keep Up

Some interviewees worried not being able to grow old grace-
fully. Although this feeling was shared by several people, the
comments centred on a pressure to stay physically young,
having babies when you didn't really want them, not retiring
when you want and the fear of dying first, thus leaving a loved
partner alone.

> We talk sensibly about when she is left a widow, but I curl
> up inside at the thought of her being left alone; maybe
> she'll blame me for dying first.

Other comments made by the older partners in our survey
might be more fairly classed as irritations than significant disadvantages. For example, the younger partner's occasional lack of
sophistication in taste or behaviour was cited:

> Even when we went to the smartest of restaurants, he
> managed to find prawn cocktail, duck à l'orange and
> some kind of Black Forest gâteau on the menu. I was
> mortified!

> Her table manners are not always up to the standard of
> my generation and it grates when she says 'Hi' instead of
> 'How do you do'.

Disparities in income were also mentioned, as in this case by the
younger gay partner, who says:

> I am sure that my relative lack of resources was a problem
> for him. He didn't mind paying but he'd have felt better I
> know if our income had been more equal.

The fact that many age gap relationships establish themselves
and are then maintained is concrete demonstration that the

partners within them find many advantages in such relationships. The comments above show what some of the advantages (and often their complementary disadvantages) are. The level of enthusiasm expressed about age gap partnerships has encouraged us to try to summarize what there is to be gained from being in such a relationship.

The Gains

The advantages of such a relationship are many. To start with, one of the partners is bound to have a great deal more experience of life than the other. This can be useful in a variety of ways — just dealing with the day-by-day vagaries and vicissitudes of life is an example.

> At the same time, because she is so much more in touch with the modern scene than I am, I can, at least, receive an inkling of what is going on with the younger generation. It all helps with my trying to be a bit more tolerant. We both learn about each other and our different outlooks on life together. Well, that's the theory: mostly it works out in practice. Altogether it's been a most successful marriage and now, almost 11 years later, we're looking forward to the next 11 successful years.
> (man 30 years older)

For each age gap relationship reported, the gains are obviously individual and particular to the two people involved. Nonetheless we identified three broad themes.

The Opening of Doors

When you are with your peers, their pressure, common background and outlook may ensure that a relationship runs along 'tramlines'. There are unspoken norms in the way you relate to each other and in your group. There are collective activities which tend to encourage you to stay with your peers and not to undertake activities and interests outside that group. In contrast, a relationship with someone from a different age-group can give freshness and new perspectives. You come into contact with values and experiences you haven't met before. Our interviewees talked of opening doors, of being freed from the constraints of peer expectation, and this allowed them to develop personally.

We all grow up with sets of expectations placed on us. These come initially from parents and family; later from friends and the society in which you move. Happy with this, many people never move very far out of the arena in which they first began. This remains so in spite of greatly increased geographic and social mobility. Some people do move, however. Exceptionally, they win the lottery, become disabled, or travel to the other side of the world. More frequently, dramatic and unexpected changes occur through the vehicle of relationships. Jokes are made about knights in shining armour riding up the road, but, for many of our interviewees, meeting with their age gap partner provided a change that was almost as dramatic.

> I don't think my sense of gain can be overstated. I feel I was given a whole second life — totally different — after I thought it was over. There was a feeling of marvellous unreserved bonus. She loves me for what age has made me.

Not only did meeting their age gap partner open doors that had hitherto been closed, but it also enabled those interviewed to pass through those doors by freeing them from previously held expectations. The restraints felt because of background or lack of experience were overcome by meeting this person and, because of the difference in ages and all that this meant, this particular Mr or Ms Right was able to provide new insights, offer new experiences or unlock hidden talents in their partner.

New Perspectives

Through a doorway lies a new vista. Because your partner grew up at a different time and with different cultural influences, they will view the world a little differently from yourself. This alternative perspective allows you to have greater self-awareness of your own relationship to the world. It can be very difficult to decide about a new house or change of job while you are actually in it – you need physically to get away from both your old and new home, or go on holiday from your job to be able to make a sensible judgement about what action to take. This can also apply in relationships, and such a perspective may be easier for couples where there is an age gap between them.

It may also assist communication. Communication is an essential element in building and maintaining a successful relationship. The obvious age disparity may encourage couples to talk about themselves and the relationship more than a non-age gap couple would. You cannot be oblivious to this disparity and rarely did these couples just drop into the relationship without talking about the issues involved. Many same age couples manage to do just that! Our experience, having interviewed so many people, suggests that age gap partners probably talk to each other more. The high standard of communication we found in age gap relationships will, of course, make them more confident and willing to be interviewed!

The ability to communicate well starts with knowing yourself and knowing where your own reactions and emotions have come from. The older partner may already be confident about talking, or they may have had bad previous experiences of not talking which they do not want to repeat. For the younger partner, the new perspectives may encourage greater self-awareness. These were not necessarily desperately serious matters, and included new hobbies and pastimes:

> I had never been to the theatre apart from to see a pantomime, and here I was at Glyndebourne – it was amazing.

or new sets of friends and different conversation:

> Her friends seemed so easy discussing feelings and were quite challenging to me about mine ... It scared me, but I liked it.

or new ways of having sex:

> I was older and should have been more experienced I suppose, but her sex life had been so much freer than mine because she'd grown up in a more permissive age, so it certainly gave me lots of new ideas.

Just sometimes did they offer a whole new way of looking at life.

> I have to say that she changed my life, my way of looking at things, my confidence, the way I viewed things, the way I judged things. I divide my life into BC and AC (Before and After Caroline). Before her, I was a suburban chap with a suburban outlook. After her, I hope I'm much, much different.

Whatever these new perspectives were, they constituted a great gain for both participants. Older partners were shaken out of old routines, and were able to catch up with newer attitudes or trends, being tempted into activities conventionally outside those accepted for their age. Younger ones were exposed to experiences they might otherwise have taken years to acquire, if at all.

We both experienced enormous gains in the relationship, but that's because of who we are, not how old we are. It's a very long list . . . We seem to have arrived at the same stage of personal development and have similar needs.

Being loved like that — adored totally to madness with a totally satisfying sex life — gives you a confidence you never lose — lets you know your life has not been in vain. You are no longer looking and searching. You know what it is.
(woman 22 years older)

Hybrid Vigour

True gains in a relationship must come from both sides: a gain for one partner should not constitute a loss for the other, but be balanced. For many age gap relationships this is often true — we were told of the mutual benefits of the partnership. We've labelled this 'hybrid vigour'. If you are a gardener, this may be familiar. For us, it is an analogy we feel is enlightening if we are to understand the success and attraction of age gap relationships. In the plant world, hybrid vigour is the phrase used to explain the particularly vigorous growth that often occurs as a result of breeding two different subspecies of a plant. The offspring frequently grows much more strongly than either of its parents — as anyone who has a Leyland cypress hedge will know! We are not making an exact analogy since we are not referring to the children of the relationship, but to the partners themselves. Nonetheless, the union of two people with very different ages and backgrounds can generate a relationship which is infinitely stronger than the sum of the parts. In dealing with the world, the sum of the experience of age gap couples may be greater than many equal age couples.

Together we make a formidable combination: my grey-

haired wisdom with his youth and ebullience. It makes for an exciting time, but also for one which is so productive somehow. I know that we will have the same values always but what still takes me by surprise is his ability to show me an extra dimension to a subject. Similarly, I know he finds not only comfort in my grey-haired wisdom, but learns and develops from it.
(woman older by 17 years)

Perhaps the unrecognized possibility of this extra vigour is another attraction of these relationships. Of course sometimes the vigour comes from the greater physical energy of the younger partner, but it is important to realize that there is such a thing as intellectual vigour and, beyond that, what we might call experiential vigour – namely, the strength that can come from age and experience, which was so valued by our interviewees.

I would change nothing about the relationship. It was like a gift to me from the cosmos, from God – from the other world – Avalon – a blessing – a privilege. I am eternally grateful.

8

Achieving a Successful Age Gap Relationship

Looking for Mother or Father?

The most significant element of an age gap relationship is the relationship, not the age gap. This fact is overwhelmingly clear from our interviews. Yet every relationship is difficult to maintain, and needs hard work from both partners if it is to survive. To choose a partner who is visibly outside society's norm, who is probably at a different stage of emotional, educational or professional development and who is likely to have the different view of life that each generation develops from its precedent, would appear only to stack the odds further against maintaining a successful relationship. So what might age gap couples be looking for in making such a choice? And how might such relationships work 'against the odds'?

Even the most self-aware amongst us are often far from clear about the motivations behind our actions. We might have a rough idea, as did these two interviewees:

I had always been a tall girl for my age (at 13 I was 5'11"). I never resented this at all, but I always felt completely stupid with boys of my own age and I am sure it worked in reverse.

One of my reasons for taking an interest in older men was really my desire to be untypical ... The very least I could do, to satisfy my desire not to be doing what was expected, was to have relationships with older men.

On reflection, this initial notion reveals a more pressing motivation, however:

> I had always been thought of as being much older than I
> was – more worldly, sophisticated, experienced than my
> years would imply. I think this was the result of a lot of
> reserve on my part, having been made to feel pretty
> worthless at home and therefore being afraid to divulge
> my true inadequacies. I always sought in a partner
> someone who could make up for this, someone who
> really knew what everyone else thought I knew, someone
> whose example I could follow without having to admit to
> the outside world that I 'didn't know'.

> There may be a deeper reason that demonstrates the need
> for acceptance rather than the need to rebel. As a child
> and teenager, I never had great success with my peer
> group, and used to take comfort in being on good terms
> with my teachers. Also my parents' friends and the
> parents of my friends used to like me a lot ... it was
> certainly easier for me to make relationships with them
> than with members of my peer group.

But we do not choose our partners in an entirely rational way.
We look for someone who will best meet our emotional needs.
Reflecting on her older partners, one interviewee summed this
up as follows:

> I look back with pleasure at these two relationships and
> owe a lot to both of them. They were lover, father, guru,
> mentor, friend to me.

We don't need these elements equally, nor for all our lives, but
we do need aspects of each role at different times. The particular package of roles we need our partner to play for us is
shaped by our childhood experience and remains with us

throughout adulthood. This applies just as much to age gap relationships as to more 'normal' partnerships. But the difference is that age gap couples believe that someone much older or younger will provide their best match. Why might this be?

The popular response would be that 'They are looking for a father- or mother-figure'. Of course, it takes two to tango so must there be an equal number looking to *be* a father or mother? If there is a hoary old chestnut with respect to age gap relationships this must surely be it and no writing on the subject can avoid it. We feel that such comments are made partly because an age difference is so immediately obvious, while similarities of outlook and background are much less clearly discernible. But there is likely to be truth in it, although whether they were seeking a parent/child more than other couples is quite another matter. In our view, almost all couples are looking for some parenting in their relationship. But the parenting role should be shared, so that each partner gets a turn of either parenting or being parented, as is appropriate to their needs.

Why Look for a Parent?

As we said above, the package of roles we need our partner to play for us is shaped by our childhood experience. Why childhood? Because our infancy is the most influential period of our lives. It is when fundamental character is set and whatever your situation was at this time will have an influence on your life. The issue is not whether that upbringing will have had any effects, but what those effects will have been. Since the most intimate relationships we ever have are with our families, a child's family exerts an especially dominant influence. Divorce, remarriage and step-families may have ensured changes, but 70 per cent of children are still with both their parents for the first five years. Observation of this one parental model is easily assimilated as the only model for our own adult relationships, and it strongly influences our choice of partner.

As a striking example, the daughter abandoned by the father will always be affected by this event in some way. In adult life she may unconsciously repeat the pattern, even though she tries to escape it. The boy whose mother was cold and distant may, as a man, seek to compensate by marrying a warm outgoing woman, only to find her overbearing. He resents her wanting to be so close to him because he has had no practice in such situations.

Both our mothers were younger than our fathers (11 and 20 years). Neither of us had had any other age gap relationships but I suppose it felt comfortable to both of us to be with someone where the gap fitted our parental pattern. This occurred to me at the time but I didn't know what to make of it — I suppose I just thought it was an extra dimension of closeness. Thinking about it rather worried me as well, because the obvious thing that people say about age gap relationships is that you are looking for a parent. I don't think this is necessarily so at all but it bothers me that, because my father died, I might have been doing this whether I realized it or not. I'm very uncomfortable with this thought and, in any case, the relationship wasn't at all parental. I think sexual relationships always are, to some extent, and this can be very good and very comforting, but if anyone was the parent in this sense, it was I as the younger partner.

The fact is my father did leave my mother when I was 7 and I didn't see very much of him when I was growing up so, yes, I have an issue with my father and that was reflected in my relationship with Andrew.

Where they have not been sufficiently well mothered themselves, someone may be seeking a partner who will be a mother.

Barbara who is 30 years older than Peter, is mistaken when she says:

> His own mother died when he was 8 months old so he can't have been seeking a mother-figure in me because he had no idea what a mother was.

Some who choose older partners are seeking a parent figure and are aware of it:

> Although I have had just as many relationships with men of about my own age, those in which the man was significantly older than me had, as it were, an added dimension. It's quite simple, really: I've always liked having a father-figure; so, in these partnerships, the normal man/woman relationship was overlaid with a child/parent one. In fact, I was particularly attracted by men who already had children, because that seemed to add somehow to the 'father' image that I liked to conjure up. It was a turn-on for me.

We are not implying you can never get away from your child-hood pattern or improve on that of your parents. You can. But what happened to you as a child, particularly how you learned about relationships, will affect your own participation in them later.

What Aspects of Parenting Are Especially Relevant?

The assumption that the parent and the child roles will always be taken by the older and younger partners respectively is quite wrong. To be at the grandparent stage of life does not necessarily mean you have the skills required of a grandparent. Nor does it mean you have lost the need to be a grandchild. Older partners, by virtue of their age, may not necessarily be experienced in relationships or used to the rough and tumble in them.

> I was almost 20 when I married the first time, a man some 20 years my senior. This was a disaster; not because of the age difference but because years had not given him the maturity and kind of experience I needed and intellectually we were on a totally different level. Although I left him four years after we were married, I think I realized on my wedding night that I had made a dreadful mistake.

A lover is not a parent, although some elements of parenting exist in all good relationships. All those with an older partner are not necessarily seeking a parent. Consider the experience of Amanda and her older partner, for example:

> It would be easy to see her as my mother and it is true that I badly needed one because I have never got on with my own mother. I do need Amy to look after me in some ways but in fact I don't think it is as a mother. I notice how she is with her own son and daughter and she does not over-mother them; she is very laid-back. Also, in a way I feel I am the parent, if anyone is, because I was the one who knew I was gay first, felt comfortable with being different and was quite happy to sever all contact with my family this year.

What Does a Mother- or Father-figure Give You?

Many remarks made to us about 'only looking for a father-/mother-figure' were said pejoratively, as though seeking such a figure were in some sense a failure. Yet good parenting is an immensely nurturing process, which enables you to grow and mature. Good parenting, the best kind of parenting, does not try to keep you in the same emotional place.

Some elements of parenting did appear to be particularly sought by age gap couples.

Repairing Damage

A relationship may enable a healing process to take place, repairing damage from earlier in life.

What is it that a child needs when it has hurt itself? It will run to a parent and hope to hear the words 'Mummy/Daddy will make it better.' If you have had a particularly difficult or damaging experience in a previous part of your life you may have some special need which is not met in a 'normal' relationship. This is not to say that all those who go for age gap relationships have been damaged, but they may, through the bad experience, have developed sufficient awareness to locate the type of partner most likely to 'heal' them. The different perspectives, experiences and skills encountered in an age gap relationship are outside the normal experience of a relationship with a person one's own age, and these differences make the prospect of repairing damage a reasonable expectation.

The relationship just corresponded to my emotional needs, in other words, a need for a father-figure coupled with the desire to live on my own with only a part-time relationship. From his point of view, I suppose, like so many men, he preferred to have a sexual relationship with a younger woman rather than someone of his own age. But then I don't think he was as aware of the age difference as I was. For both of us, what we were doing was healing the wounds we had gathered in previous relationships.

Security

We all hope that our parents will give us security while we are growing up and finding our place in the world. Many of the people entering age gap relationships that we spoke to were seeking financial and emotional security:

> All of my relationships have been with older men, the minimum age difference being 13 years. The need for security engendered in me a preference for more stable men, men who were not just starting out in life, unsure of themselves, still suffering the impatience of youth. Having received much verbal abuse from both parents from age 5, I was always seeking relationships in which I was encouraged to find myself, to be myself with a partner who was sure of themselves, who was not still finding their own way ... Perhaps I was looking for a husband who had some value to make up for my inadequacies.

> My wife has no hang-ups, emotional or otherwise. She is well-adjusted, in fact very grown-up — that is why I married her.
> (man younger by 14 years)

> I don't deny that I like the good things of life and he is well-established in his career, so we can have them.
> (woman younger by 15 years)

But a word of warning ...

Power and Control

Although it is the nurturing, safeguarding, secure elements of parenting which some people may value in their age gap relationships, there are other less nurturing elements of parenting which some age gap partners clearly seek. These are the more controlling elements. Those contemplating an age gap relationship should either be wary of these elements or try to sort out why they may be seeking them in the first place.

Parents do hold power over us, but we gradually challenge this power as we grow up and eventually take control of our own lives. The holding and exercise of power within age gap relationships could be particularly significant because it may be more easily unbalanced than it would be in an equal age relationship:

> He held me back, he made all my decisions for me. He was good at being a father-figure but was too powerful.

A parental relationship is, psychologically, a powerful one and as well as the younger partners who might be looking for a parental figure, there have traditionally been many older men who are looking for younger partners. In fact, this may be the immediate image that springs to mind when the phrase 'age gap relationship' is uttered: the middle-aged man with the glamorous younger woman on the arm. The young woman may be needing a parent and the older man may be searching to be a parental figure by exerting and demonstrating power over his partner. At the same time he hopes that she will confirm his continuing virility, thus showing his peers that he is still powerful.

The role and value of this type of relationship would seem to be that of giving a message to the external world – much as an expensive car or house might do – rather than one of providing support and sustenance to the partner. It is an unrealistic expectation on the part of the powerful partner – traditionally the man, although of course powerful older women can fall into the same trap – to presume that their partner will remain submissive and willing to be controlled.

It is all very well being married to someone hugely

successful but not if you harbour ambitions in the same direction yourself.

What often happens is that the power and money given to the (female) younger partner increase her confidence. She then begins to assert her identity and independence and starts to grow as a person. She no longer fulfils the role of the submissive partner, which is what the man wanted, so he ceases to want to know her. This pattern may then lead him to seek another subservient woman, and so the cycle continues.

Older partners of either sex, therefore, should heed this warning;

> There can be relationship difficulties, and these are increased when one of the people is the other's protégé. Usually this is the younger person, but anyway the one disadvantaged by class, education, skills or whatever. Once the protégé 'grows up' or reaches anywhere near the standpoint of the 'teacher' and finds their own voice and opinions, the 'teacher' usually becomes very angry and jealous.

Good parenting does not try to keep you in the same emotional place but helps you to grow and to become powerful yourself, so that over the years the balance of power between parent and child shifts until a balance is achieved when the child reaches maturity. This is not easy to achieve, and it can be just as difficult to find an appropriate balance of power acceptable to both partners in an intimate relationship. This is an issue that probably requires explicit discussion and one that is best initiated by the partner who most obviously holds the power. NB Self-awareness required!

> Power between us was hopelessly unbalanced and I think now this had a lot to do with age. I found it hard to argue with him, not only because his intellect could sometimes

be intimidating, but because I was instinctively more respectful of him than of someone younger. He has far more money than I do (a new situation for me) and paid for lots of things all the time. Since he was so much richer and older, I didn't have much trouble letting him, but these are all issues of power and control, which he had and I didn't. It took a long time, and was very difficult, to see him as an equal and assert myself.

The power thing – I realize this is a very blunt and unromantic way of looking at relationships but it's necessary, although you can't generalize because power issues depend so much on individuals. I don't know if a relationship with an older woman could be more equal than ours but I do think it must be an area of potential difficulty and, surely, the bigger the gap, the greater the likelihood of the kind of imbalance.

Does All This Matter?

We have looked at the mother/father component of relationships because this is the aspect of age gap relationships which is uppermost in most people's minds. Yet not all our interviewees went into these complex reasons why they took up in their age gap relationships. Most people do not analyse their reasons for entering relationships like this and tend to give rather more straightforward reasons. They do not offer the information that they are seeking to repair emotional damage, to find security or exert power, but we hope our interpretations of their motives may prove enlightening in some way.

Given the delightful idiosyncrasy of individual human beings, we could never hope to explain all the motives behind all the partnerships we encountered. There will be interlocking motives behind the interaction of every such couple and they may meet their needs in ways that other types of relationship would not. They may have greater needs than others for the nurturing and security which comes from parenting, but those needs are fulfilled by how they relate together as a couple rather than in the simplistic way in which they may be viewed by society.

From our contact with people who have joined up 'across the years', our impression is that they related together successfully, in spite of the obvious discrepancies. Are there special reasons why this should be so? Are there differences between these and all other relationships which might also be defined as successful?

Successful Relationships

Defining a successful relationship is fraught with difficulties, but a good starting point would be one which lasts, which gives happiness to both participants and in which both partners have the opportunity to grow and develop emotionally. An initial framework for success is to check what people are seeking from any committed relationship. If you ask your friends what they want from a relationship, they are likely to come up with three key ingredients:

- *Shared values* – common understanding and standards of behaviour and background
- *Shared interests* – home, children and friends once the relationship is established
- *Support* – the knowledge that your partner will always be there for you in times of trouble

However, these may be expressed more in terms of 'We think the same', 'He is always on my side' and 'We have a lot in common'. Age gap relationships are little different from all others in these respects, although, as we saw in Chapter 2, they may have several distinctly 'non-shared' values. Generally the differences in background and experience could be used beneficially for the relationship.

We may look for these factors, but to achieve successful relationships depends on three further elements, which are particularly important in age gap relationships.

Expectations

Each partner will have realistic expectations of the other. This not to deny romance, but expectations based merely on romantic hopes are usually doomed to failure. For instance, no amount of romance surrounding the fairy-tale wedding of the Prince and Princess of Wales could overcome their basic incompatibility. If your expectations are too high, you will not only ensure that you are constantly disappointed but will also guarantee that your partner feels they are always falling short of what you want and need, therefore creating feelings of inadequacy within them. Some feelings of inadequacy are acceptable in a relationship, but a person who feels inadequate all the time does not function well either as a partner or as a supporter for someone else.

> It wasn't so much the years between us as the fact that his feelings of being not quite a whole person got in the way of any relationship. He was too hard on himself and expected too much of me, too.
> (older woman)

Conversely, most of our interviewees felt that they were able to have realistic expectations of each other, even in very difficult circumstances.

> I met my husband 22 years ago and he is 20 years my senior, but after all this time I cannot say that I notice it

... He gave me a stability I had never had before, and I could always call on his advice and help without ever feeling inadequate or stupid. He has always encouraged me in whatever I felt I wanted to do. For the last nine years, following a total hysterectomy, I had the most severe and crippling symptoms yet he never complained, and supported me in my conviction that the cause of my virtual inability was indeed physical. I think a man of equal age, 37 at the time it all started, would really have looked elsewhere.

What is important is not so much the nature of the expectations themselves but the fact that they are understood and accepted by each partner. We were offered some less than usual examples in the course of our interviews. One 'solution' was to spend considerable time apart:

We always have and still continue to meet every other night and weekends. In the past year he has taken to staying over at the weekend. We go on holiday together, too, of course. But we are so comfortable together, like a pair of old and comfortable slippers. We have never had a row or disagreement – there doesn't seem to be anything to have a row about! Which, of course, means that the sex is wonderful and just gets better and better and better. (older woman, after seven years)

Another 'answer' was to live much of the time in different countries:

After living with Alex for 18 months and feeling a bit that I had settled into retirement at 25, I fulfilled a previously held ambition to go and live in Berlin for a while. Three years later we are still together, living in separate countries, which seems to suit both of us very well. I can live out my fascination with East Berlin, and enjoy the youth

I missed out on (because I was too busy swotting for exams), and he can work undisturbed at his computer in London, free of my jibes about him about becoming a Mac-bore.

These expectations may be unusual but they are practical and realistic for the individuals within their own relationship.

Communication

Successful relationships are based on good and open communication. The ability to share thoughts and feelings, to talk about things which are difficult, and to do so at a stage before a crisis has been reached, could be the most vital ingredient of a relationship.

Many couples only talk about really important matters at the stage where it is almost too late for talking. There are many reasons for this; lack of practice, not knowing how to find the words, not wanting to rock the boat by raising a difficult issue; perhaps, above all, lack of time and opportunity in busy lives, when the urgent drives out the important. As one interviewee said of her previous relationship:

> I lost track of how many times we got to a point late at night when we had admitted something was bothering one of us and the other one would say, 'Let's talk about it in the morning.' Of course, we never did and the only time we ever talked in the morning was on the day he told me he was leaving.

As we said earlier, many age gap couples appear better at this communication business purely because there is an age gap. You are less likely simply to drift into such a relationship and may be forced to face obvious differences before a partnership can be established. You may also be pushed into defending the relationship to outsiders, and this also encourages a couple to discuss the partnership between themselves. Many older partners are more self-aware and confident about talking, and, of course, our interviewees were likely to be even more comfortable with talking!

Good communication was not always the case and a few older partners used their power to avoid it. This unsettled their younger partner:

> He was a very mysterious person. He was so secretive about his past that it was just something that I couldn't touch. I never really knew what he did as a job, although I eventually sort of got to the bottom of it but sometimes I wouldn't know where he was — it was a very dysfunctional relationship.

Keeping things to yourself in this way can help retain power but does not do much for communication. An overwhelming majority of our interviewees felt that they enjoyed better communication in their age gap relationship than in any others they'd experienced.

> Because things seemed stacked against us, with me being so much older than he is, we had to talk and talk and talk when we first decided to make it permanent. I am glad to say it is a habit which has never left us.

Compromise

The people whose relationships last and develop are individuals who possess the right level of willingness and ability to make compromises. This does not mean that you have permanently to accommodate your partner's wishes. On the contrary — you will often need to stand your ground and set limits. One partner should not always be the one who compromises or gives way. Both should have, or be willing to learn, the art of negotiating so that a balance is achieved between each of their needs. This can be as trivial as deciding which kind of take-away to have on Friday night:

> I don't like Indian but will put up with it every other week as long as he lets me have all the Tandoori chicken.

or the music played at home:

> I love jazz, hate opera and he is the opposite, so we listen to show music and are both happy.

or, more important, such as where to go on holiday:

> When the children were young we always had beach holidays, which I know he hated, so now I'm happy to go on walking holidays and when I am desperate for some sun, I go off with a friend for a week to a Greek island.

or as fundamental as what happens in the bedroom:

> I know he wants me to smack his bottom with a whip but I just can't bring myself to do that. Now and again I'll spank him with my hand and he seems quite happy with that.

The essential element is that those involved are willing to:

- understand and accept the other's needs even if they don't share them
- negotiate around them
- come up with a solution or means of dealing with the problem which satisfies both parties

We believe that when couples live together successfully and happily you will find that all six of the above elements will be present, i.e.

- shared values
- shared interests
- mutual support
- realistic expectations
- open communication
- willingness to compromise

These apply to all partnerships and, provided you have them, you need not worry too much about the age difference. In fact, you may be even more likely to find them with a much older or younger partner.

In the end, does it matter what the motivation is? Do you need to know? Not necessarily, though it will probably help you manage your relationship better if you have some idea of what you are looking for within it. Of course, you may seek something quite simple yet find something quite complex and far-reaching, as did one young man we know of:

John was the child of a family which had fallen on hard times and lost its middle-class status both because of problems in the family business and because of the illness of his father. John himself left school at 16 and went to work as a clerk in a local Town Hall. The job neither interested nor inspired him, but the family needed his contribution to its income especially as his father's health deteriorated and his mother's time was increasingly taken up by looking after him. The family home in a poor area of London was not a cheerful place and John missed the attention he had enjoyed from both parents at an earlier stage of his life. One day, when John was about 20, a new neighbour moved into the flat opposite. She was in her mid-thirties and had been separated from her husband for several years. She had a son and daughter, both in their teens. Before very long, John became a regular visitor to her flat, which seemed a haven of warmth and fun to him after the rather bleak atmosphere of his own home. Jean was a very attractive woman but also a wise and mature one. Their physical relationship blossomed, a major feature for John in the restricted society of the 1950s, but he gained other things from the relationship, too. Jean mothered and cosseted him, made him feel good about himself. She developed his confidence in himself. Although nearer in age to her children than to her, he became a surrogate father to them and he felt good that Jean, an experienced parent, turned to him for advice about her family and valued his opinion. Oh, and she did his washing and cooked him meals, too, which his mother, now taken up with her caring responsibilities, had been neglecting of late.

Jean did something much more significant for John, too. Like a concerned mother, she took an interest in his career and encouraged him to better himself. She suggested he got a job in a bank, coached him for the interview and when he landed the job insisted that he should not be content to stay on the first rung but should do the banking exams so that he could progress. Crucially she also made him join the political party of which she was a very active member. In a short space of time he had become a member of the local council and was progressing up the political ladder as well as the business one. As John's confidence developed, it was perhaps natural that he should grow up enough in the relationship to feel he had no more need of it. The relationship wound down by mutual consent and the partners went their separate ways. Whenever Jean sees John now, as Prime Minister of Britain on TV, does she enjoy a frisson of satisfaction about her part in his development? And does John think warmly of Jean and acknowledge how important a role she played for him? We like to think so.

9

Advice

We asked our respondents to offer advice to others in a similar situation to themselves; either those entering such a relationship or attempting to maintain one. There was often initial hesitation:

> I'm not much into giving advice to other people. I think I'd just say that if you are compatible, and the prospect of unequal dependence doesn't daunt you, then age is immaterial.

But this slight reluctance was quickly overcome, and their advice to potential or actual age gap partners can be summarized as follows:

- Go for it! To hell with the consequences and with what anyone else thinks; you won't regret it. Trust your instincts.
- Think long and hard and if you are happy about various aspects, then OK. These aspects include ageing, caring, differential development.
- Proceed with extreme caution because the risks may outweigh the benefits.

They also gave practical advice on the handling of an age gap relationship for those still determined to proceed.

Go for It!

My advice to anyone about to embark on a relationship with an older partner – providing he isn't attached – is go for it! Every week in the *Guardian*'s lonely hearts column, I see eligible men who just want some company, and young girls who can't find Mr Right. There is an army of girls like me, seeking a more mature and spiritual relationship than we are getting from our peers. Likewise, there is a corresponding sea of lonely bachelors not daring to approach us for fear of being scorned. Life's too short to sit and wait. There would be a lot less heartache if people would overcome their fears and prejudices and communicate with each other across the years.

The only advice I could possibly give someone about to embark on such a relationship is trust your instinct. That is what I did and, even in the times when I was less than completely happy, I did not regret having done so.

We were struck by the energy and feeling of sheer joy which frequently accompanied this advice. Naturally, it came most often from those who had had good experiences in their age gap relationships, but even from those who had not been completely happy, there was a strong feeling that what they had learned and gained in the relationship was of immense value and that they would not have missed it for the world.

The only real advice to someone embarking on an age gap relationship – if you love each other, age really doesn't matter.

If you have two years of happiness or more, you will have achieved more than most marriages.

I am so happy and content that, if anybody else contemplated a big age difference relationship, I'd say, 'Why not, if you really love one another it doesn't matter in the slightest.'

It is not surprising that some of those who expressed the 'go-for-it' view were influenced by their sexual experience in the relationship. Their feelings of exhilaration were palpable, as we learned to recognize. One described

The sheer unexpectedness of finding those sexual feelings at a stage of my life when I thought it was all over.

and advised:

If sex is offered to you, take it. Drink it in. Eat it up.

There were also some reservations:

If it's just for sex, I'm not so sure . . . Not all young men are as mature as Liam was at 15. If an older woman wants to 'play', she could do more harm than good from embarking on such a relationship. We all know about fatal attractions!

But they didn't only mean sex. In contrast to other relationships, this particular one had offered greater opportunities for communication and sharing. They had often overcome difficulties and pursued the relationship in the face of opposition, and this led them to value it strongly. The experience of being 'two against the world' also stimulated strong feelings of closeness and togetherness:

My advice is to enjoy the time you have together providing you can cope with the remarks and behaviour of others. People will always view your age gap with

concern or seaside mentality, assuming that the benefits are stacked in the older man's favour. But remind these blinkered people that life comes with no guarantees and, if you are happy together now, what is the point in being miserable apart for the rest of your lives?
(woman 15 years older)

What advice would I give? None. Maybe I was lucky, I married a man who just happens to be a bit older than I am. I could have married a man who was my age but was mentally very old. I really do not think that age has much to with whether a relationship is a happy one or not. Sometimes in the small wee hours, I do think, if only he could be more . . . or he could be less . . . but I believe that if I was given the wand, I would not wave it. If he was made to change, then he would not be the man I chose to spend an awful long time with.
(25 year gap)

Most of the time I don't even think about the age gap. It should certainly not be a bar to an otherwise fulfilling, trusting, loving and honest relationship where the sex is good, too. I'd say that the same age is the least important thing for two people to have in common.

Think Long and Hard

This set of reactions was more cautious, acknowledging the difficulties. The advice was still to go ahead but that potential problems should be recognized and considered before doing so.

If asked to give only one piece of advice I would suggest: Think long and hard about the future. It may be wonderful now, but will you still be able to hack it in 5, 10 or 15 years time, when the perceived age gap will undoubtedly widen horribly and without warning?

I'd say to a younger man contemplating an older age gap relationship, think very hard in respect of her in later years, but if she's good fun and easy to get on with – go for it. She'll love and cherish you in a way not possible for a young woman.

People were encouraging, but realistic:

Any advice I would give would be encouraging, but I would also try to suggest an eyes-open approach, to acknowledge that there is a discrepancy. It is vital to strike a balance between rejecting society's pressures (even more intense if the woman is the older party) whilst accepting that there is a real difference which cannot be wholly and for all eternity consumed by your passion.

There was awareness of the problems which families could cause. Sometimes they opposed the relationship itself:

I think my family's opposition to him forced us together. Everything became more intense and I felt propelled into marrying him because they were against him just on the grounds of his age alone. In retrospect, they were maybe more sensible than I realized because now he is an old man, whereas I'm still energetic and lively.

Other family elements, notably step-children, brought stresses as well. As we have seen in Chapter 4, these can be of particular significance in age gap relationships.

Had I realized just how hard her kids would make it for me, just how rejected I'd feel by them . . . I don't know. (younger man)

Interviewees who suggested proceeding with caution were aware that while everyone should be realistic about what they can expect from relationships, those embarking on an age gap one should be more realistic than most.

The plain fact is that all relationships are difficult to maintain over a protracted period, without any specific extra burdens of difference of class, background, education or colour, and an age gap falls somewhere in this category.

I would advise someone starting a relationship like mine not to assume that the partners understood one another without checking. Things have different significance to different people and I think the bigger the gap between you, the more different your assumptions are likely to be. Romance can make you feel totally at one when you're miles apart, and you don't even notice. The whole relationship with Ian was incredibly romantic and we wrote poetry for each other and did all kinds of things that I'd always wanted to do but with someone else would have felt silly. There was a formal quality to it all – like a courtship – which absolutely swept me off my feet, and which seemed entirely in keeping with Ian's personality, but would have seemed very odd in somebody my age. Some of the things he said were beautiful and unforgettable, and the hardest thing when the relationship ended was having to accept that they hadn't meant to him what they mean to me. I can't tell how much of that was due to age and how much to just being different to each other.

If you are looking for a father, fine, but just bear in mind that that may rather restrict his ability to be the lover who sweeps you off your feet also.

Proceed with Extreme Caution

Here, the down side of these relationships was made apparent. Sometimes, like this older man, this was vehemently expressed:

> The gap association does differ from all other relationships because of the element of child-parent, parent-child, and no doubt it owes much of its excitement to that fact. If it is intended to be permanent, it is fraught with problems over and above the natural difficulties of most couples, and in general terms it is better avoided. A more sophisticated view might well be that if it can be experienced without too much pain or damage to either party as part of a life, then why not – but not as a likely formula for success. My advice to someone about to embark on such a course is quite simply, except as a passing experience, don't. You are stacking the cards against yourself.

This younger woman felt worn down by the amount of caring she'd found herself with:

> I simply never realized when I was swept off my feet by that powerful and compelling man that I would end up cleaning up his incontinence. The Parkinson's disease has taken him over and he is a different person entirely. We had some good years together, which I wouldn't have wanted to miss, but if you ask me if they were worth what I have to go through now, I'd have to say no. Is that terrible? Anyway I know it is not necessarily because he is older that I'm in this position but that feels like the reason and it makes me cautious about recommending such a course to anyone else.

This woman regretted not listening to her friends' advice:

They knew I would be hurt and warned me, but I ignored them until it was too late and I was hurt.

And this younger man didn't regret his experience, except that:

The problem is she spoilt me for any other woman. I keep looking for one like her who is 25 and in reality you can't be like her at 25.

For the younger partner in a relationship, there was the cautionary warning that:

I would tell them to look at an older partner's track record particularly carefully, because if, by a certain age, you haven't sustained a relationship, there's some reason for that. You can be unlucky in love in your early and middle twenties, but not for a quarter of a century, and I think you reach a point where you don't know how to be close to another person and it's too late to learn.

Not to mention the warning about being too young to make decisions for the rest of your life:

I was 21 at the time of our wedding and, with hindsight, green, naïve and wet behind the ears. One year at 20 is only a twentieth of a life, and perhaps only half of their adult life, if that. How can one forecast feelings that you will have at the age of your parents, never mind later. Would I advise someone else? No, but I'd be longing to say, 'Don't on any account,' because of the problems with sex, friends, children and, not the least, the changes that are natural in the younger partner's developing life.

Even for those who advised extreme caution, there was an understanding that decisions about relationships are rarely taken rationally.

If only we really could be sensible about these things. But emotion 'recollected in tranquillity' is really only in the poet's mind, isn't it? The other idea maybe we should cling on to is that it is not the experience which matters anyway, it is only how you use it.

Practical Advice

Quite apart from the principle of entering an age gap relationship (or not), several interviewees offered practical advice for those who do go ahead. These included the consideration of where you live:

Have a tenants-in-common agreement if you share a house.

They also suggested that you make sure you have hobbies which will bridge the age gap:

As for any age-group, a shared sense of humour and a hobby are the two basic essentials for any relationship.

You must understand the need to maintain independence within the relationship and recognize that older people may need more independence than if you and your partner were of a similar age:

Economic independence, so one can maintain a separate identity and lifestyle alongside that of the partner . . . i.e. more like a single.

This included keeping separate sets of friends:

The advice I would give, and have been giving lately to a

19-year-old friend going out with a 38-year-old man, is to keep your own lives going, have independence and keep contacts with your own age-group, which is where your friends, pre-relationship, are likely to be. Introduce your partner, and try not to make them too aware of the difference in age; play it down. After all, if you want to be with a guy who is so much older, then age really doesn't matter, as your wanting to be together stems from attraction and similar tastes. There are no age barriers.

The interviewees also suggested that help should be sought at an early stage:

I'd advise that it is worth getting counselling when things start to go wrong.

This particular person felt that he would never have given such advice when he was younger:

I thought I knew it all then, and that asking for help would have been admitting failure, but Lorna has helped me to see that it is not. Her generation has a different view of these things.

There was practical advice, too, about preparing for the situation — which might well arise — when one of the partners, usually the older one, becomes frail and needs care.

I wish we had thought to take out some kind of insurance at a much earlier stage, which would have helped us buy in care when he had his stroke. Because he was older, we should have foreseen that this might happen and if I could have had a break or a bit of regular time off it would have stopped me getting quite so frazzled.

The benefits system is complex and difficult to find your way around so it is worth finding out what your entitlements are at an early stage. Arrangements can then be made for any property to be protected for the benefit of the younger partner or for assets to be arranged so that the maximum amount of help can be accessed.

As far as step-parenting was concerned, our interviewees again advised seeking help at an early stage from others who have had similar experiences, or from professionals. They counselled strongly against trying to replace the absent parent in any way.

And, if not actually practical advice, several people made the comment that

A shared sense of humour is an essential ingredient for a successful relationship, I'd say.

Our Advice

I don't think one can make general points of advice to people starting relationships. The last thing people want when they get involved with someone is dark warnings about the possible consequences.

It *is* notoriously dangerous to advise people on their relationships. Indeed it could be argued that, in respect of our love lives, almost none of us take advice! We may ask for it, may clamour for it from friends, but what we are often actually seeking is confirmation of what we believe, feel, or are doing. We want practical advice that will help us pursue the course we are taking – we want to know how best to succeed in pursuing X – not to be told that he or she is the most inappropriate and damaging choice of a partner we could ever have dreamed up!

Many people were shocked at our decision to marry. I suppose they thought our relationship was a fairly casual deal which would fizzle out, exhausted by the blindingly obvious unsuitability of the two of us. Only a few exceptions made their reservations known. I don't think anyone could have affected my decision at that time, and once I had decided to marry I did not go through a lot of questioning or nerves about my decision.

The only advice any one of us is really likely to take is our own. Therefore we'll present our advice as a series of questions for you to ask yourself.

Before doing so, if we were to attempt to distil what we have been told by our interviewees, it would be something like this:

Change is inevitable in relationships. Don't think everything will always stay the same, because it won't. You may not be able to control the change but you can try to ensure that you will each change in a way which keeps you compatible. This leaves particular difficulties for age gap couples, because not only do you start out with a more than normal set of differences between you, but the very entering of the relationship may itself bring about changes which you did not anticipate.

I was undeniably middle-aged and set in my ways, whereas Jo was developing late and on an exponential curve of progress towards the maturity she'd missed out on earlier ... I would certainly warn any prospective age gap partnership about the likelihood of such a development.

You have to try to equip yourself for these changes and others which may happen in any relationship.

In summary, our advice is:

- *Talk, talk, talk* – there can never be too much communication.

- *Compromise* – if the relationship is good enough, surely it is worth a little give and take.
- *Know yourself* – the best contribution anyone can make to any relationship is to be aware of what you yourself want and need from it, and what you are able to give to it in return.

Here are the three questions you might ask yourself about your relationship:

Are You Expecting Too Much?

Anyone embarking on a relationship needs to keep their expectations realistic. The two interviewees below realized – too late – that they were not doing so:

I would have changed a great deal. Perhaps given my partner more of a sense of humour and inner security, and myself more maturity. I should have worked harder on a shared social life. I believed at 23 I could do it all: work, be my own person, get on with his kids, win his ex-wife over, keep house, look good, support my partner and be a good daughter. I learned that for me all of this was not possible.

He once said to me, 'I hurt for the lack of love in my life,' which I found heartbreaking and made me want to give him the love he lacked but I failed to recognize that this didn't mean he would welcome me or be able to take a partner's needs into account . . . I had no sense of what it is like to be in your middle forties with your life established to the point where change becomes unwelcome and finally impossible. My assumption has always been that I will eventually enter a lasting relationship whereas James has given up the hope of this. This was a huge difference between us ... His attitude seemed to be that it was too late for him to change, and now I actually agree with this. I think it is difficult for anyone to really change, but for a man in his forties who has always been alone, to be with another person on a deep and meaningful level is just not possible, perhaps even if they want to be. He was so unused to considering the needs of another person. If being 'past your sell-by date' means anything, it means this – that you've had one kind of life too long to adapt to another.

As several of our respondents pointed out to us, warning bells should sound for you if you find a potential partner who has reached middle age without ever having lived with someone or made some kind of commitment to a relationship.

The younger partner should ask why their prospective partner is still single and whether they have the experience and capacity to commit to a partner relationship. You might distinguish them from divorced or widowed people, who have at least a track record of living with someone. You need not be entirely depressed by the lack of track record: it doesn't mean they can't have a relationship; just that it can't be the same kind of relationship they'd have had at 21. They have to match your expectations of the relationship not only with their own, but, more crucially, with their ability to fulfil those expectations. Don't let the fact that your proposed partner is older delude you into thinking that age of itself gives you solid experience of relationships. It does not, as this mother wryly pointed out:

I would not urge anyone into a relationship with an age gap over 10 years. At 23, I said to my mother, 'Look at Bogart and Bacall – it worked.' I remember my mother laughing and saying, 'He ain't no Bogart, he's not got that much going for him and you're not as tough as Bacall was. They are the exception that prove the rule.' She had a point.

It might also be a good idea to acknowledge the comments of friends, even if you don't agree at the time:

> I think actually I should have listened to my friends a bit more. I think there's this big problem that friends have when they think you are in the wrong relationship. They think they can't say anything and at one stage I was close to marrying him, and that would have been a total disaster, and yet I was I very unwilling to accept any of their sort of 'Clare, are you sure this is right?', and I think I should have listened to them a bit more because they were proved right in the end.

Are You in the Right Place Yourself?

Everybody knows about the dangers of making relationships on the rebound. The fact that everyone knows this does not, of course, stop them doing it: witness the fact that 80 per cent of divorced people who remarry do so within two years of the first marriage ending. However, it does mean you are vulnerable;

> How can one really give advice to another person embarking on any relationship? Any partnership is like an adventure and has to be worked at. If either partner has been in a previous relationship, there is also a period of healing that has to take place, which can last for a considerable time. I didn't leave it long enough.

This vulnerability may go back further. Where severe childhood deprivation for both parties is involved, it pays to think at the outset what the underlying emotion is. It's all too easy to confuse love with compassion, particularly when the differential is of father/daughter or mother/son proportions.

But there are other times in your life when you may be particularly susceptible to an age gap relationship and from the experience of our interviewees we would suggest a degree of caution. Consider Liz, for example:

> I was very unsure of myself and didn't know where my career was going and it was a time I was really unhappy at work and that was probably all to do with it. I was working way out in Haslemere and I had to commute out and get up early and it was really miserable.

Several other interviewees were in their mid-twenties, unhappy or dissatisfied when all the attractions of an older partner were persuasive. But because they didn't go in feeling equal, or feeling belief in themselves, it was not a relationship based on respect for different qualities but one in which the younger partner was the 'child'. All that happened was that they ended up feeling exploited.

> But although Tony hurt me very badly, I partly blame myself for this because it should have been obvious from the start that he was not looking for the same kind of commitment that I was. Looking back I can see it very well, but obsession with him prevented me from seeing it at the time, because I so much needed him to be the right one.

If you are feeling very insecure, ask yourself if you are looking for an older person just because age itself seems to give that air of security? If so, beware on two counts. You may not have constant need of a protector, it may just be a temporary thing. Second, the older person is not necessarily able to give you security just because they are older. They, too, may be looking for a protector. Is that what you want, too? Are you willing to be one?

> I think it is important that the younger one has at least reached their twenties. One changes so much in one's

teens that the younger person is unlikely to be the same person five years later. Otherwise, I think one probably risks the same triumphs and disasters as any other relationship.

If a younger partner is looking for security, the older one should ask if they are looking to boost their confidence by displaying knowledge and power.

> Just because you are older, don't think you know it all. You can learn from your younger partner too, you know. Neither should you feel you have to take the responsibility.

Are You Using the Age Gap as a Catch-all Excuse?

It is an easy trap to presume that all the differences between you and your partner can be put down to the age gap and therefore ignored. The normal rules of a relationship apply here too. Don't think that all the rules which apply to equal age relationships will be irrelevant if there is a large age gap: the importance of culture and background, for example.

> I did not realize that I was Sheraz's first ever non-Turkish partner and I realized gradually that he would never seriously consider commitment or marriage with an English woman. This stunned and hurt me and was the single most important reason why the relationship failed.

There isn't a different set of rules applying to age gap relationships. Some things may apply less forcefully but differences in race, culture and class need to be addressed as carefully as they would be in any other relationship.

> I was English, he was a Latvian-born US citizen; he had left

education at 20 (over 20 years before), I had just graduated. He was too close to his retired working-class parents; I was still very involved with my own professional parents. He was brought up in suburban America of the 1950s and 1960s, I in central London. In addition, he was introvert, quiet; I was gregarious and people-orientated.

The age gap was likely to be the least of the problems for the relationship described above, which foundered after marriage. So, to repeat a message in different words, however great the gains from an age gap relationship, they are unlikely to overcome adversities that would wreck the most stable of marriages:

It was as if the things which brought us together served in the end to drive us apart. In absolute terms the startling difference in our age, and therefore our expectations of what life should be like, were stimulating at best and at worst irrelevant (or so I thought). It is hard to admit it, but the ordinary pressures of a highly stressful life did eventually destroy our inspiration. Living in a tiny shoebox, expensive apartment, trying to run a business together, constant financial anxiety and no free time, were all major factors in our demise. The irrepressible force which brought us together in the first place does still exist but not in any practicable form.

Having said that we were reluctant to give advice, of course we have ended up by doing so. But, to make ourselves feel less guilty about appearing didactic, we will leave the final word on advice to two interviewees:

I would recommend any woman marry an older man . . . if he's not fossilized in the past, if he's adaptable, if she loves him, if he's more than a generation, say 20 years, older than she is. There's no competition between Brian and I, and I think that's because there's 30 years between us. That gap is large enough to promote tolerance. I don't expect him to act like a man my age and he doesn't expect me to act like a woman of his age. We laugh and have fun and do all the serious things like earn the money and allocate scarce resources — age has nothing to do with it.

On the whole, I'd say, if you want a real roller-coaster ride of a relationship, need someone with a stable outlook, intelligence, knowledge and love, don't just limit yourself to your own age range — open your mind and you might just find a piece of paradise. Who wants a 'normal' relationship?

10

Future Trends?

So what have we learned about relationships which span a wide age gap?

First, that it is the relationship which is important, not the age difference. There are certain elements to be extra-careful about if you are embarking on an age gap relationship, as we showed in Chapters 7 and 9. But if the main features of a good relationship exist, you have just as much chance of making an age gap partnership work for you and your partner as any other kind. Indeed, since the elements of communication and realistic expectation may be stronger than in an equal age relationship, you may actually stand a better chance of happiness.

Second, we have learned that what people seek in an age gap relationship is the same as anyone now, or generations before us, have always sought: the love and security of a partner. The immense changes in society brought about by technological and other developments have not affected this basic fact. However, the freedom of people to move geographically and socially may mean they are now better able to meet prospective partners outside their normal social group. This increases the likelihood of age gap relationships coming their way.

This is probably no great surprise. What is more directly significant for age gap relationships is that their numbers are increasing — yet not in the traditional way of older men marrying younger women, but of older women marrying younger men.

Figures from the Office of Population Census and Statistics on marriages in the UK for 1979 and 1992 were as (overleaf):

Younger Women – Number Marrying Men 16+ Years Older

Total	Woman's Age										
	−20	20–4	25–9	30–4	35–9	40–4	45–9	50–4	55–9	60–4	65–9
1979											
6,336	833	1,414	1,243	1,080	678	409	320	186	124	42	7
1992											
5,938	340	1,376	1,597	1,011	622	437	327	103	86	26	13
As a percentage of all marriages for that age group											
1979	1.08	0.94	2.15	3.5	4.16	3.69	3.95	3.27	2.98	1.4	0.3
1992	2.26	1.35	1.74	2.37	2.91	3.05	2.99	1.81	3.12	1.24	0.93

Source: Office of Population Census and Statistics 1979, 1992

Younger Men – Number Marrying Women 11+ Years Older

Total	Men's Age										
	–20	20–4	25–9	30–4	35–9	40–4	45–9	50–4	55–9	60–4	65–9
1979											
2,291	154	601	549	393	182	129	109	90	54	21	9
1992											
3,034	145	862	916	585	231	124	75	29	35	18	14
As a percentage of all marriages for that age group											
1979	0.65	0.41	0.63	0.91	0.86	0.92	1.08	1.19	0.86	0.54	0.26
1992	3.73	1.24	0.89	1.06	0.85	0.68	0.58	0.36	0.67	0.76	0.59

Source: Office of Population Census and Statistics 1979, 1992

In summary, these figures show the numbers of older man/younger woman marriages to be similar in 1979 and 1992, while those between older women and younger men have increased by almost a third over the same period. This increase is despite a 15 per cent decrease in the overall number of marriages for the same period. Not included in the figures above is the unsurprising evidence that by far the majority of age gap marriages are second marriages for one of the partners. These are the only definite figures. But many age gap couples may be living together without being married. Given that these are likely to be second relationships for many, and that many others will be deliberately childless there is an argument for expecting a higher proportion of age gap relationships not to be formal marriages. The figures (directional), therefore, underestimate the actual number of age gap partnerships.

Are there any reasons for the figures above? How are traditional views changing?

The Traditional View

People seek the same things in age gap relationships as they do in any other: love, security and support. Seeking a relationship with someone older or younger often has additional motives. For older men, these have included:

- the need to reaffirm their 'pulling power' by having a younger woman on their arm
- the need to seek a new lease of life once a long-established marriage has ceased to bring excitement: the traditional mid-life crisis motive for men
- the need to prove their virility by having a second family

For younger women, the reasons for seeking an older mate have included:

- the attraction of men in more powerful positions than their peers.
- the financial security offered.
- the greater emotional maturity of the older man.

For older men it has often seemed very acceptable, even desirable, for such relationships to flourish. Although there has always been a varying measure of disapproval about situations where 'she is young enough to be his daughter', it has often been seen as a normal course of events. This is related to the experience of history. In mid-Victorian times the average length of a marriage was 12 years and death ended marriages in the way that divorce does nowadays. It was expected that, when a man's wife died in childbirth, he would take another wife and she would very often be much younger so that she could provide him with a second family. The problems associated with step-parenting are clearly not confined to the twentieth century! Whether or not such relationships are approved of may reflect a society where, broadly speaking, the rules have been set by men.

Meanwhile, relationships where the woman is the older partner have been far less permissible. Public fascination with cases in which older women have relationships with men or boys much their junior is highly evident. Major taboos still exist over such liaisons:

> If it had been a man of 40 with a girl of 16, people would have tut-tutted but understood both of them. The other way around is still considered unacceptable.
> (Claire Rayner, agony aunt, commenting in 1994 on a case of an older woman marrying a man much younger)

Until comparatively recently, sexual relationships were made respectable because they led to procreation: thus a relationship where the woman was older and either beyond or almost beyond child-bearing age did not fit easily into that expectation.

Changing Patterns?

In recent years there has been greater anecdotal evidence of age gap relationships and particularly of those with a woman as the older partner. This could have much to do with the increasingly titillating nature of the British popular press, which has taken more frequently to reporting such relationships or covering them in a more salacious way to increase sales.

Yet there are definite changes afoot. While the older man/ younger woman relationship, with its established pedigree, continues in the same numbers in the UK, there are changes where the older partner is a woman.

What are the reasons for this change? And what pattern may lie ahead? Do the statistical changes reflect changing attitudes?

Changes for Women

Since long-term relationships no longer have to be based on marriage, has this freed people to have age gap relationships when they would not have thought of actually marrying that person?

It may be a completely different matter entering into a short -term or even a longer-term relationship with a so-called unsuitable partner rather than having to commit yourself to marrying one. This may also be the explanation for the phenomenon of down-dating (*see Chapter 6*).

The news that actress Glenn Close was to marry a carpenter and that Liz Taylor had married a truck driver is part of the recognized phenomenon of down-dating or BOR (bit of rough). Well-heeled and successful women have no need of an acceptable man, especially one who pays the bills and expects to call the tune. If you are giving *him* a clothing allowance – that says a lot about you! It certainly shows the world that not only are you independent but you are able to keep a man rather than be a kept woman. It also proclaims to the world that you are having great sex, because why else would you keep him? It may shock your friends but they'll probably envy you, and it will definitely cause a stir, which most of us like to do now and then!

As more women become more powerful, do they attract younger men by that power, in the same way that older men attract young women?

The men who are the subject of down-dating are attracted to women who are more powerful than they are, and clearly for many of them it is a turn-on.

If one of the important elements in a relationship, especially an age gap one, is the attraction of power, then it is logical to assume that as women develop more economic and social power, more young men will be attracted to them, not only for the turn-on of power itself but because of the financial security which it can offer to the partner.

As more couples feel free to choose not to become parents, does this mean they are free to have relationships which will not lead to parenting?

Because there is, for women, unlike for men, a limit on their child-bearing years, this may have been one reason why partnerships between older woman and younger men have been traditionally less acceptable. Society now seems more accepting of the idea that not all couples want children, admitting that maybe you can be happy and fulfilled without reproducing yourself, even perhaps acknowledging that children put too much stress on a relationship, rather than bolster it. Is it, then, more acceptable for women to be with younger men, now they are not judged purely on their potential reproductive capacity?

Despite medical discoveries extending the child-bearing years of women well into their fifties, recent research shows that one in five women in Europe will remain childless all their lives. Today's older women are effectively the first to benefit from control over conception in their earlier child-bearing years. So they may be freer to choose to dedicate themselves to a career when their family is grown up. Today's younger women may be choosing, in much larger numbers than ever before, not to have children at all.

As women's overt sexuality has become not only more accepted but positively celebrated, does that enable them and their partners to choose relationships where sex is an aim and not incidental?

It would once have been absolutely unacceptable for a woman to say openly that she simply wanted sexual gratification from a relationship. This has always been for men something which is at worst acceptable and at best something to be admired. If you pick up a women's magazine these days, you may well get the impression that women want nothing else, so great is the emphasis on improving the quality of your orgasm and achieving the best sex life ever. The phenomenon of the Chippendales and similar male strip/dance groups also suggests that it is acceptable for women to do what has previously been seen as the prerogative of men; to be openly turned on by looking.

Such an example of this is the coverage of older women going to the Gambia on their holidays, either for temporary companionship or in some cases to acquire a permanent younger partner, however unsuccessfully in the long run. The Gambia has been a popular UK holiday destination for some years, offering the essential holiday requirements of beaches and fine weather all year round at a reasonable price. Amongst those holidaying in the Gambia there has developed a substantial group of older single women who are travelling specifically to find younger companions. They are doing what countless men have done before them – taking a sex tour to a foreign country. Until recently, this would have been an unheard of thing for a woman to do, although it is well known that men seek the solace of much younger women on trips to the Far East.

Travel agents do not actually run sex tours to the Gambia, but somehow it has become known that it is a place which is reasonably accessible and until recently politically stable. There is not only sea and sand, but a ready supply of available young men. One couple who went there reported:

We were surprised on the plane out there to see how many women in their forties and fifties were on the trip. At first we thought they must be an organized party from a club or something. Then it dawned on us that they were all travelling alone. When we got there at the first evening 'do' we all attended together, there were lots of giggles, etc. and we became aware that the waiters and so on were sort of expected to pay attention to the women and take them out. One told us that a friend of hers had, as she put it, 'taken one home with her' and was going to marry him.

This phenomenon would not be new or even surprising for men, but it is a little unusual when it comes to women. This may well be a growing trend, as women begin to feel more open about their sexual needs, more confident about saying they want sexual gratification and have more money to buy themselves such holidays.

It may not be solely about sex, however. For women, it may also be about finding reassurance and encouragement about their appearance and sexuality after years of marriage where self-confidence and self-esteem was progressively run down. Travel agents planning for the future have perhaps taken note.

Medical and Social Changes

These have enabled women to stay physically younger for longer. Huge numbers of women now take hormone replacement therapy (HRT) to counteract the symptoms of the menopause. You take a pill and you stay younger longer, or so the story goes. Certainly the number of well-preserved looking women in their fifties and sixties owes a lot to HRT. It also owes a lot to different lifestyles, of course. Women no longer slave over a hot stove or a dolly tub but switch on the microwave and the washing machine instead. As a consequence, they do not look as worn as their grandmothers did.

It is hard to remember, when I think of my grandmother, that she was in fact under 40 when I was born. She always seemed old to me and she was: she had false teeth, grey hair and wore slippers. She hardly ever left the kitchen in fact. I am much older now than she was when I was a small girl, but I would never dream of having false teeth or grey hair, and I'm too busy screwing my young fella to go into the kitchen much.

In summary, the economic, social and medical developments in Western society have enabled a wider group of women to make choices about their personal lives in a way that was never possible before. They are divorced from their husbands, have enough money to enable them to pursue some of their ambitions, and feel able to take a younger man as a partner. They can do this without societal disapprobation or the disapproval of peer group and contacts in a way that would not have been possible for previous generations of women.

These changes for women and the difference in how they are viewed have inevitable knock-on effects for men.

Changes for Men

In an age where men may live in fear of being branded sexist, are some more reluctant to be seen with 'bimbos'?

A good proportion of men nowadays live in fear of being called politically incorrect because of their attitude to women. Many a chap fears giving up his seat or walking on the outside on the pavement. Might some of them, therefore, also fear of being taken less seriously by their peers because they do not have what is seen as a serious companion? There is probably enough pressure on some men that counterbalances the number who do take a 'trophy wife'. This may explain why the number of older men marrying younger women is stable rather than increasing.

Do men now in their fifties and sixties have a traditional view of 'the little woman' which young women find increasingly unacceptable?

Many women, both younger and older, seem to find the attitudes of men difficult to accept. They do not want to be 'sitting at home with the slippers', as one put it to us, whereas older men, however reconstructed they seem, may carry those expectations deep down because these are the ones with which they were brought up. It is hard to 'unlearn' attitudes learned at your mother's knee, yet many women now find these attitudes unacceptable.

As the Child Support Agency in the UK, and equivalents in other countries, make the responsibility for first families a permanent commitment, will men be less able to take on second families? Such legislation receives wide public support when it is introduced, and is evidence of society's view of the ongoing responsibilities of being a parent.

At the very least men are likely to think more carefully before they take on a second family. Society, quite rightly, is beginning to legislate upon its strong disapproval of men who leave their families to the care of the State or to that of an unsupported wife, while they themselves make a fresh start with a new wife and a new family.

Where is This Leading? Watch This Space!

With the trend for women to feel freer to have relationships outside what have hitherto been considered the norms, and with more pressures on men which may militate against going into the younger woman scenario, we can expect a greater balance in future. It will be seen as much more run of the mill for women to have younger partners than for men to do so, as has been traditionally the case in the past.

In California, for example, an organization called Mutual

Admiration has been extremely successful. This singles service aims to bring together 'Sophisticated Attractive Older Women and Younger Successful Men who empower each other'. Weekly parties are held in trendy clubs and restaurants: for $12 you enter a world of ageless-looking women aged between 40 and 60 and young men in their twenties and thirties who cruise around looking good, swapping phone numbers and making dates. So successful has it been that it is to be launched nation-wide as Passions Voice, and is to become a public company.

We cannot draw conclusions about major societal changes from the relatively small number of people to whom we have spoken. Nonetheless there are straws in the wind which do suggest that a revolution may be under way in the manner with which relationships operate 'across the years'. If so, it will require a major rethink for many people. We suggest that anyone interested in the phenomenon watches the trends care-fully, but not so carefully that they stop enjoying what one of our respondents called

The roller-coaster ride of an age gap relationship.

Index